T0135766

Design and Programming of Reconfigurable Mesh based Many-Cores

Dissertation

A thesis submitted to the
Faculty of Electrical Engineering, Computer Science and Mathematics
of the
University of Paderborn
in partial fulfillment of the requirements for the
degree of *Dr. rer. nat.*

by

Heiner Giefers

Paderborn, Germany
Date of submission 06.03.2012

Bibliografische Information der Deutschen Nationalbibliothek

Die Deutsche Nationalbibliothek verzeichnet diese Publikation in der
Deutschen Nationalbibliografie; detaillierte bibliografische Daten sind
im Internet über http://dnb.d-nb.de abrufbar.

ISBN 978-3-8325-3165-2

Logos Verlag Berlin GmbH
Comeniushof, Gubener Str. 47,
10243 Berlin
Tel.: +49 (0)30 42 85 10 90
Fax: +49 (0)30 42 85 10 92
INTERNET: http://www.logos-verlag.de

Abstract

Over the last years, the semiconductor industry has rapidly moved away from high-frequency designs to multi-core architectures in order to increase the performance of processor chips. No other reasonable way than increasing the level of on-chip parallelism has been found to exploit the opportunities of technology scaling. The term "many-core" was coined for architectures which incorporate dozens to thousands of individual processing elements. Even though the construction of many-cores is not a technological challenge, the success of many-core devices is so far hindered by the lack of widely accepted parallel programming models. Sequential programming is still dominating, but the advent of many-cores will certainly force programmers to start making their programs parallel to gain performance. To this end, clear and easy programming models are required in order to support the programmers writing parallel applications.

The reconfigurable mesh is one model for massively parallel computation that was introduced in the late eighties. A reconfigurable mesh consists of an array of processing elements and segmented buses between these elements. Each processing element has an associated switch which can be reconfigured to connect the segmented buses such that different global communication patterns are formed. Although the model attracted high interest and was a subject matter of intensive research, it has not been fully established for practical use. There are several reasons for this development. The model poses the assumption of a constant time communication delay between arbitrarily distant nodes. Additionally, the model was investigated at a time when the performance gain of single core microprocessors was largely satisfying. Today, the preconditions have completely changed. It is feasible to manufacture chips with several hundreds of processing cores, fast on-chip networks reduce global communication delays. A reevaluation of the reconfigurable mesh model under practical considerations could reveal considerable advantages, because the erstwhile practical limitations have become less critical.

The goal of this thesis is to investigate the reconfigurable mesh as a programming model for many-cores. To this end, I present methods for generating, programming and debugging reconfigurable mesh architectures based on soft processor cores of different granularity. As the reconfigurable mesh has mainly been used as a theoretical vehicle, issues of programming tool flows have not been sufficiently considered. For this reason, I develop dedicated programming flows for the proposed many-cores. The new programming language ARMLang allows for the specification of lockstep programs on regular processor arrays, in particular reconfigurable meshes. Using FPGA prototypes and the presented programming flows, I provide new practical results for the reconfigurable mesh model. By means of various case studies I show how reconfigurable mesh algorithms can be conveniently programmed and compiled. I also provide new insights into the aspects of algorithmic scalability, fault tolerance and power management for reconfigurable meshes. In order to extend the communication capabilities of the reconfigurable mesh interconnect I create a light-weight, packet-switched Network-on-Chip.

With this thesis I provide the first ever practical study of word-level reconfigurable meshes implemented in FPGA technology. Although the communication delay is not constant as assumed by the model, my results show that algorithms scale well on the implemented prototypes. Extensions like an ultra-fast barrier network or a dedicated power management mechanism further improve the efficiency. Taken together, my work provides a framework for studying reconfigurable mesh architectures and the presented case studies demonstrate the pertinence of the model for future many-cores.

Zusammenfassung

Weil sich die Leistungsfähigkeit von Prozessoren allein durch Miniaturisierung und Verbesserungen der Mikroarchitektur kaum weiter steigern lässt, baut die Halbleiterindustrie seit einigen Jahren auf Multi-Core Architekturen. Bereits heute ist es technisch möglich, mehrere hundert Rechenkerne auf einem Prozessor zu integrieren. Diese Prozessoren nennt man auch "Many-Core", da sie sich konzeptionell von Prozessoren mit nur wenigen Kernen grundlegend unterscheiden. Um Many-Cores effizient nutzen zu können, müssen vor allem Antworten auf zwei wichtige Fragen gefunden werden: Wie können diese Prozessoren effizient programmiert werden und wie kommunizieren die einzelnen Kerne untereinander?

Die Art der Kommunikationsinfrastruktur hat einen großen Einfluss auf die Wahl des Programmiermodells. Ein Programmiermodell, das massive Parallelität vorsieht und Rechenkerne durch ein spezielles rekonfigurierbares Netzwerk verbindet, ist das Ende der achtziger Jahre entwickelte Reconfigurable Mesh. Ein Reconfigurable Mesh besteht aus einem regulären Gitter von Rechenknoten, wobei jeder Knoten aus einem Prozessor- und einem Switch-Element besteht. Die Prozessoren können aufgrund lokaler Entscheidungen das Schaltmuster des zugeordneten Switch-Elements umschalten und so globale Kommunikationsmuster einstellen. Für dieses Rechenmodell wurde eine Vielzahl von Algorithmen entworfen, deren Laufzeitkomplexität der sequentieller Alternativen deutlich überlegen ist. Bisher hatte das Reconfigurable Mesh vor allem theoretische Bedeutung, denn einige Modellannahmen waren bisher technologisch nicht zu realisieren; so etwa die Annahme, dass Daten im rekonfigurierbaren Netzwerk in konstanter Zeit übertragen werden können. Durch aktuelle Entwicklungen in der Halbleitertechnik werden diese Einschränkungen immer weniger kritisch. Es ist bereits heute möglich, hunderte von Prozessorkernen auf einem Chip zu integrieren und über extrem schnelle Netzwerke zu verbinden. Somit sind die Grundlagen für eine praktische Umsetzung des Reconfigurable Mesh Modells immer mehr gegeben.

In der vorliegenden Arbeit untersuche ich das Reconfigurable Mesh Modell auf seine praktische Verwendbarkeit als Architektur- und Programmiermodell. Dazu entwickle ich Konzepte und Werkzeuge, um Reconfigurable Mesh basierende Many-Core Prototypen zu generieren und zu programmieren. Meine Ergebnisse stützen sich auf zwei verschiedenartige Prozessorkerne die jeweils als Prozessor-Element eingesetzt werden. Für beide Alternativen stelle ich dedizierte Programmierflüsse vor. In diesem Zusammenhang ist auch die neue Programmiersprache ARMLang entstanden, mit der sich parallele Programme für Prozessor-Arrays entwickeln lassen, die auf Instruktionsebene synchronisiert sind.

Auf Basis von FPGA Implementierungen und den vorgestellten Programmierflüssen werte ich die vorgeschlagenen Architekturen anhand einer Vielzahl von Fallstudien aus. Weiterhin präsentiere ich neue praktische Resultate zu Aspekten, wie der Skalierbarkeit von Algorithmen, Fehlertoleranz und Energieeffizienz. Um neben Reconfigurable Mesh Algorithmen auch Programme unterstützen zu können, die eine weniger reguläre Art der Kommunikation erfordern, kann das Reconfigurable Mesh Netzwerk um ein paketvermittelndes Netzwerk ergänzt werden. Meine Resultate zeigen, dass je nach Kommunikationsmuster eine Alternative überlegen ist und dass sich durch die kombinierte Nutzung beider Netzwerke die Leistung des Systems steigern lässt.

Mit dieser Arbeit stelle ich die erste FPGA-Implementierung eines auf dem Reconfigurable Mesh Modell basierenden Many-Cores vor. Dabei zeigt sich, dass die Reconfigurable Mesh Programme auf den Many-Core Prototypen gut skalieren, obwohl die Annahme, dass Kommunikation in konstanter Zeit erfolgt aufgrund technischer Gegebenheiten nicht strikt eingehalten werden kann. Praktische Erweiterungen, wie ein spezielle Synchronisationsnetzwerk oder Mechanismen zur Minimierung der Verlustleistung erhöhen die Effizienz der vorgestellten Systeme. Die vorgestellten Methoden und Werkzeuge zeigen, wie sich das Reconfigurable Mesh Modell für Many-Cores nutzen lässt und stellen darüber hinaus eine wertvolle Grundlage für zukünftige Untersuchungen dar.

VI

Contents

List of Figures

List of Tables

CHAPTER 1

Introduction

1.1 Motivation

Gordon Moore's famous prediction that the number of transistors placed on an integrated circuit would double every 18 to 24 months has held true for almost 50 years and will presumably hold true for several years to come. Until only recently, the shrinking of transistors and, as a consequence thereof, the reduction of supply voltage could be roughly translated to increases in clock speed and microprocessor performance. A second performance gain spurred by Moore's Law were the microarchitectural improvements which could be implemented with increasing transistor count. But since about ten years ago, both strategies to increase the performance of microprocessor chips were pushed to their limits. First, microarchitectural improvements have been yielding diminishing returns and second, more importantly, ever-increasing clock frequencies have lead to dramatic power dissipation problems.

Increasing the degree of on-chip parallelism has been identified as the only efficient way to scale performance while keeping the processor's power consumption within a certain budget. This lead to a dramatic change in the architecture of processors and systems. Almost any of todays computing platforms, either embedded or general purpose, is multi-core. In the embedded domain, System-on-Chip became standard, i.e., designs in which multiple and, in large parts, specialized cores operate together on a single die. In the field of desktop processors, we see an increasing number of general purpose cores integrated to multi-core chips.

In common terminology, multi-core refers to chips with multiple homogeneous processor cores in one microprocessor package. Typically, the independent cores are connected via a bus system and share the same global memory. Due to their architecture, shared memory multi-cores are very well suited for the multi-threaded programming model. Although writing multi-threaded code is not trivial and difficult to debug, multi-threading is the most widely accepted way of parallel programming and operates well with cache-coherent multi-cores. However, the majority of the research community as well as leading industry experts predict that the number of cores will increase dramatically. With a much higher number of processing cores, techniques which work for multi-cores are no longer feasible. As such chips are fundamentally different to multi-cores, a new term many-core was established for these processors.

But what exactly distinguishes many-core from multi-core? First, as sharing a global bus for communication does not scale for a large number of cores, many-core needs a new communication infrastructure. Second, it is not known how to efficiently program processors with several hundreds of cores. Both issues, the programming model and the communication infrastructure for many-cores are of great interest and importance in the computer science community and serve as a motivation for this work.

A particularly much-discussed topic is the question of suitable programming models for massively parallel systems. We know how to scale the number of cores, but we do not yet have software that could utilize the cores efficiently. Legacy code is sequential and it is difficult to automatically extract parallelism from it. It is even proven that only modest amounts of parallelism can be obtained for programs with complex control flow [92]. To exploit massive amounts of parallelism, explicitly parallel programs are essential. In contrast to sequential processing, where the von Neumann model serves as a unifying model of computation, there is no prevalent programming model for parallel machines. The reason why such a singular parallel programming model is difficult to find lies in the diversity of parallel computers.

For many-cores, the way how processor cores are connected to each other has a great influence on the programming model. Today, Networks-on-Chip are accounted as the most promising interconnect architecture for many-cores. The Network-on-Chip paradigm applies concepts from high-performance off-chip networks to single-chip multiprocessors. This principle makes Network-on-Chip a very general communication architecture and also makes it possible to directly adopt programming models from the domain of distributed computers. But the generality of Network-on-Chip is also accompanied by disadvantages, for example, a usually higher communication latency. Data must be wrapped into messages and the routers have to analyze meta information in order to forward the packets. For that reason, Networks-on-Chip tend to be not optimal for fine-grained parallel applications because they require fast and seamless communication paths.

In the past, several massively parallel models of computation like the Systolic Array [91], Pyramid and Hypercube networks [95] and the Reconfigurable Mesh [113] were developed, all of which are based on dedicated fast interconnection networks. For these parallel models and architectures, a vast amount of algorithms was created, most of them dramatically reduced the runtime complexity for the targeted problem compared to sequential counterparts. So far, not many of these models attained sustainable success in commercial or practical designs. However, as Moore's law proceeds, single-chip implementations of massively parallel processors will become more and more feasible and thus, it is of great relevance to practically review the "old" massively parallel models under the new circumstances.

This thesis contributes a review of the reconfigurable mesh model of massively parallel computation for many-cores. The reconfigurable mesh model relies on ultra fast communication – in fact, single cycle communication – among cores that are connected through a reconfigurable network of segmentable buses. Constant time communication is, from a physical perspective, unrealistic as communication speed is bounded by the speed of light for any known technology. From a more practical point of view, though, the assumption becomes more and more realistic as we can put more processing nodes on a single chip and realize core-to-core communication with fast intra-chip links. With this development in mind, the reconfigurable mesh could be a practical programming model for future many-cores rather than a pure theoretical framework. Using the reconfigurable mesh programming model involves to specify algorithms in a proper way. As the segmentable bus interconnect style of the reconfigurable mesh is interesting by itself I further explore this network architecture for not only reconfigurable mesh algorithms. While being inappropriate as a general purpose communication architecture, the reconfigurable mesh interconnect serves well for certain communication requirements and here even outperforms commonly preferred Network-on-Chip interconnects.

1.2 Main Contribution

The paradigm shift towards many-core parallelism poses a multitude of issues and challenges to be addressed by the research community. Two main questions are, how should the many processors on a single die communicate to each other and what are suitable programming models for the novel architectures? In this work, I tackle both questions by reviewing the reconfigurable mesh model of massively parallel computation for many-cores.

The main contribution of this thesis is the design, implementation and evaluation of a many-core architecture that is based on the execution principles and communication infrastructure of the reconfigurable mesh parallel programming model. The novelty of the presented work lies in the fact that reconfigurable meshes, although being exhaustively studied as a theoretic parallel model, are barely analyzed under practical aspects. The specific contributions are summarized as follows:

- In this thesis, I study the potential of working reconfigurable mesh architectures that do not rely on a single cycle broadcast and quantify the results against traditional single core and multi-core solutions. I have designed and evaluated FPGA implementations of reconfigurable mesh architectures. To the best of my knowledge, this is the first practical study of word-level reconfigurable meshes implemented in FPGA technology. On the basis of industry standard soft processor cores and self-developed switch elements, the proposed design flow can be used to generate and program a variety of many-core processors. Existing theoretical results in the domain of reconfigurable meshes are extensively considered and aspects like scalability and fault-tolerance are tackled by several case studies.

- I have designed and developed ARMLang, a language and compiler for fine-grained many-cores that rely on a single program, multiple data (SPMD) execution model and a reconfigurable mesh interconnect. In contrast to the very few prior proposals of reconfigurable mesh programming models, ARMLang does not rely on a specific reconfigurable mesh model nor on a strict single instruction, multiple data (SIMD) execution model.

- In addition to the research on practical aspects of reconfigurable meshes, I investigate many-core processors based on the reconfigurable mesh model serving a wider range of applications. Additionally to the reconfigurable mesh network, the processor arrays can be enhanced by two other networks in order to achieve higher generality and better performance. An ultra-low overhead global barrier network is able to evaluate a global synchronization in the order of few clock cycles. A second data network uses a Network-on-Chip approach with classical packet-switching. Being beneficial in opposed facets, the combined use of both networks improves the performance of the many-core.

- In this thesis, the aspect of power reduction techniques for reconfigurable mesh implementations is considered for the first time. I propose two strategies for reducing dynamic power consumption for the execution of reconfigurable mesh algorithms and provide case studies and results.

The results presented in this thesis provide several insights into practical aspects of the reconfigurable mesh programming model. It is shown, that a many-core based on a word-level reconfigurable mesh can be implemented efficiently in FPGA technology and that reconfigurable mesh algorithms can be easily specified with programming languages that provide some basic functionalities to control switch configurations and synchronicity. Compared to a low-latency and FPGA-optimized Network-on-Chip, the reconfigurable mesh interconnect is more efficient for broadcasting and multicasting operands. As they also make do with a limited overhead in hardware resources, reconfigurable mesh networks provide an innovative enhancement to traditional on-chip interconnects like Networks-on-Chip or arbitrated buses. The scalability of reconfigurable mesh algorithms is being addressed in this thesis but is also identified as one key issue to be further explored in order to make the reconfigurable mesh a more practical model of computation.

1.3 Thesis Outline

This thesis is organized as follows:

Chapter 2 summarizes related work. I first give a brief overview of parallel computing models and then I review the reconfigurable mesh model in detail. The last section of Chapter 2 presents several architectures that either utilize an interconnect which is related to the reconfigurable mesh or also use FPGAs for the prototyping of many-cores.

Chapter 3 presents a methodology for the implementation of reconfigurable mesh architectures on FPGAs. A generic switch element architecture and two alternative processing element architectures are described and an evaluation of the resource utilization for specific FPGA prototype systems is given.

Chapter 4 deals with the issue of programming reconfigurable mesh many-cores. I first give an overview on the whole tool flow, including both the hardware and the software generation process. In the detailed description of the software programming flow, I distinguish two types of many-core implementations. The first is a tightly coupled processor array in which instructions are executed in a synchronized manner. For this model, I developed a new programming language and compiler named ARMLang. In the second part, I present a scheme how to program more loosely coupled many-cores that rely on barrier synchronization.

Chapter 5 provides a performance evaluation of the presented architectures. Several reconfigurable mesh algorithms of different application domains are studied and compared to sequential counterparts. The remainder of Chapter 5 deals with practical issues for reconfigurable mesh implementations, including fault-tolerance and scalability.

Chapter 6 introduces an additional interconnect architecture for the proposed many-cores which is based on wormhole routed packet-switching, in contrast to the program controlled circuit-switching of the reconfigurable mesh. The networks are compared to each other by means of communication pattern benchmarks. A case study shows how a combined use of both networks can improve performance.

Chapter 7 deals with the important aspect of cutting down energy consumption. Based on the observation that a significant number of processing elements might not be active in all phases of a reconfigurable mesh algorithm I present and evaluate two methods for reducing dynamic power consumption.

Chapter 8 concludes this thesis with a summary and identifies promising directions of further research.

CHAPTER 2

Background and Related Work

For this thesis, related work in the domain of reconfigurable meshes is of prime importance. The first section of this chapter deals with a brief survey of parallel computing models, of which the reconfigurable mesh is one representative. In Section 2.2, I review the reconfigurable mesh including its origins, several model variations, example algorithms, theoretic complexity, scaling techniques and, finally, implementations. The practical work and the technical results presented in this thesis rely on FPGA implementations. For this reason, I also present related work in the fields of circuit-switched interconnects and many-core architectures for FPGAs.

2.1 Parallel Computing Models

2.1.1 Parallel Machine Models

For sequential computing, the random access machine (RAM) is established as a general model of computation. The RAM model abstracts from the memory hierarchy of a sequential architecture by assuming constant time access to main memory and is for this reason not very suitable for runtime estimations. However, RAM algorithms are perfectly portable as they are independent of any processor architecture and give a clear impression about an algorithm's performance in terms of runtime and space (memory) complexity. In strong contrast, there is no such widely accepted model for the domain of parallel computation. The main reason for this circumstance is the diversity of parallel architectures. Parallel machines differ in how they deal with control flow (e.g., SIMD or MIMD), memory organization (e.g., distributed or shared), processor characteristics (e.g., fine-grained or coarse-grained) and interconnect (e.g., static network with a certain topology or dynamic NoC).

In the following, several approaches towards models for general purpose parallel computers are reviewed. The first, PRAM, is a straightforward parallel adoption of the RAM model which is basically of theoretical interest. Furthermore, various so called bridging models are summarized. These theoretic models take architectural aspects of parallel machines into account in order to analyze algorithms in a more realistic manner.

PRAM The parallel random access machine (PRAM) has been developed as a straight parallel derivative of the sequential RAM [63]. A PRAM algorithm assumes a set of synchronous processors which have local memory and are connected to a globally shared memory for processor communication. PRAM models differ in how memory access conflicts are resolved. The most powerful model is the CRCW PRAM which allows simultaneous reads and simultaneous writes (one writer is randomly selected) of the same memory cell at a single time step.

The PRAM has been considered as not implementable in practice as it ignores the costs of interprocessor communication. This fact is, in turn, also a strength of the model, because the algorithm designer does not have to deal with "messy" architecture details. With the advent of chip-multiprocessors, which frequently apply shared memory, the PRAM model recently regained attraction. Vishkin proposes a workflow to develop CRCW PRAM algorithms and to transform them into explicit multi-threading (XMT) programs [164] [165]. The language XMTC implements the XMT programming model in form of an extension of standard C. A corresponding compiler transforms XMTC programs to a dedicated hardware architecture, for which an FPGA-based prototype was developed [177]. The prototype consists of 65 processing nodes including one master processor optimized for serial performance and is spread over three Virtex-4 (2x LX-200, 1x FX-100) devices on a single board. Compared to a single core solution, the case studies in [177] show a reasonable speedup for the parallel versions (from 7x to 46x). As the architecture is based on a PRAM machine, it is adjusted to operate with shared memory. The worker processors have local memory in form of registers but no private data caches. As the PRAM model expects shared data to be written back to memory immediately after a change, the memory bottleneck will quite likely limit scalability.

Although the authors from the XMT project claim to explore thread level parallelism on their machine, the PRAM model itself is purely restricted to fine-grained parallelism as it executes parallel instructions in a cycle-synchronous lock-step manner. For this reason, practical implementations should follow the *asynchronous PRAM* model presented in [67]. This model extension relaxes the execution model and allows for asynchronous processes communicating by atomic read and write operations to shared memory. Further model extensions like LPRAM [11] and Block PRAM [12] incorporate local memories to model a memory hierarchy more realistically.

Bridging Models   To tackle the shortcomings of the PRAM model, so called bridging models were proposed which take into account both, algorithm design/analysis and parallel computer architecture. The bulk synchronous parallel model (BSP) introduced by Valiant [161] consists of a set of sequential processors with local memory, connected through a communication mechanism. There is no restriction on how the communication infrastructure is organized as long as it supports point-to-point communication and barrier synchronization. Because of its message passing semantics, BSP is generally viewed as a distributed memory model, but communication can also be emulated via shared memory.

BSP algorithms proceed in terms of supersteps of three phases, i.e., (i) each processor performs computation on local data, (ii) each processor sends and receives messages to and from other processors and (iii) a global barrier synchronizes all processors before entering the following superstep. BSP also incorporates a cost model for estimating algorithm performance.

In contrast to PRAM, BSP explicitly incorporates communication and synchronization of processors and takes costs for both into account. A second difference lies in the granularity of computation. Whereas PRAM algorithms synchronously execute in a fine-grained, instruction-parallel manner, the BSP model introduces coarser-grained computation phases and uses barriers for synchronization. The coarse-grained multicomputer model (CGM) extends the general BSP model by combining multiple messages to reduce communication costs [45]. This simple modification is particularly relevant for loosely coupled systems with high communication overhead, like clusters. The queuing shared memory model (QSM) is another variant of the BSP principle, with processors also executing a sequence of barrier-synchronized supersteps. But different to the original model, in QSM processors communicate through shared memory. In each superstep, processors might execute shared memory reads, shared memory writes and local computation. A notable restriction is that data read from shared memory is only valid in the current superstep.

Concurrent writes to a single memory location are resolved by arbitrarily selecting one writer processor. LogP is another bridging model developed to provide better performance estimations by incorporating more detailed network characteristics, i.e., a capacity constraint that limits the total number of messages to any specific destination to a specific threshold and an overhead parameter capturing the costs for setting up or receiving messages [42]. In a LogP algorithm, a processor can be either in stalled mode or in operational mode. Being operational, it can process local data, submit a message to the network destined to another processor or receive a message from another processor. In contrast to the other bridging models, processors in LogP work asynchronously and are not synchronized in terms of supersteps. This could be seen as a feature that makes LogP more realistic but it also makes proofs of correctness and run-time analyses of algorithms more complex. LogP has only gained rather limited interest in the theory community, as efficient emulations among LogP and BSP (and QSM) exist and BSP algorithms are simpler to design. BSP and LogP models originally ignored the memory hierarchy. This issue is addressed by several extensions, including LogP-HMM [98], LogP-UMH [13] and the Parallel Memory Hierarchy (PMH) model [14].

Several implementations of the BSP model and its variants exist, ranging from cluster and vector machines [74] [35] to chip-multiprocessor versions [34]. Recently, deLorimier *et al.* presented a custom FPGA implementation for sparse graph algorithms that bases on the BSP model [46].

2.1.2 VLSI Models

Cellular Automaton The concept of cellular automaton (CA) was studied as early as the late 1940's by von Neumann [166] and Ulam and is one of the first parallel computation model ever. A CA consists of a regular grid of processing cells, where each cell is in one of a finite number of possible states. In each processing step (also called *generation*) each cell determines its new state based on its own current state and the current states of the cells in its neighborhood.

The attraction of CA lies in its ability to model highly complex systems in a very simple way. Communication between cells is limited to local interaction, making CA perfectly suitable for the implementation with current technology. Furthermore, multiple (even one-dimensional) CA were proven to be computationally universal and thus equivalent to Turing machines. Despite its beauty, CA did not become the prevalent parallel processing model due to several shortcomings in practical concerns. For example, as Wolfram points out in [182], there exists no general programming model to organize information processing.

CEPRA (Cellular Processing Architectures) is a series of CA implementations which is based on FPGA technology [71]. CA algorithms, specified in the high-level language CDL, can be compiled to CEPRA-conform FPGA implementations [75]. As an enhancement of the general CA model, Hoffmann *et al.* propose the global cellular automata model (GCA) [76] in which the neighborhood of a cell is not restricted to local cells and can change at any computation step. An FPGA implementation of the GCA model with up to 128 cells is presented in [73].

An early FPGA-based machine of Kobori *et al.* exceedingly exploits pipelining and reaches speedups of $155x$ for a lattice gas CA algorithm executed on a Virtex XCV1000 device compared to a 700MHz Pentium-III processor. Some examples of FPGA-optimized special purpose CA implementations are presented in [41] and [146]. A more methodical approach to implement CA algorithms on FPGA platforms and a high-level performance estimation is given in [123] and [124].

Systolic Array Systolic Arrays (SA) were introduced by Kung and Leiserson [91]. Their idea was to exhaustively utilize pipelining in high-speed special purpose parallel designs in order to overcome the I/O bottleneck. In an SA, data flows in a synchronized manner from memory, through multiple regularly connected processing elements and, finally, back to memory. Benefits and applications of SA are nicely summarized in [90] and examples of efficient FPGA implentations are presented in [106], [157] and [111].

2.2 Reconfigurable Mesh

Reconfigurable meshes are models of parallel computation that connect processing elements by reconfigurable buses, mostly in a 2-dimensional grid. Each processing element (PE) controls a local switch element (SE) that itself is connected to neighboring SEs. Based on locally computed decisions, a PE can dynamically configure the switch pattern of its SE. This way, the SEs in a reconfigurable mesh can be configured to form a multitude of global interconnection patterns. The power of reconfigurable meshes stems from the fact that computation and communication are interleaved at a fine-granular level. Typically, the nodes of a reconfigurable mesh cyclically execute the following three steps: Bus configuration, communication, and (constant time) computation.

The reconfigurable mesh model of massively parallel computation can be considered as a parallel machine model as well as a VLSI model. On the one hand, the reconfigurable interconnect can serve as a communication infrastructure for arrays of autonomous processor cores. On the other hand, many reconfigurable mesh algorithms do not utilize powerful processing elements and rather compute by analyzing the signal flow through the reconfigurable network. In this approach, the reconfigurable switches act as gates or multiplexors in electronic circuitry. The parallel machine model approach is of greater relevance for this thesis However, the following section provides a broad summary of the reconfigurable mesh model.

2.2.1 Origins

One of the first projects to propose a highly parallel multiprocessor with a configurable interconnection structure is the CHiP architecture [149]. Processing elements are connected at regular intervals to a switch lattice. Each switch in the lattice has local storage for individual configuration settings. This way, the switch lattice can be pre-configured to support certain interconnection "skeletons", e.g., a mesh pattern at memory location one, a binary tree pattern at memory position two, and so on. At the beginning of a processing phase, a global controller broadcasts the memory position of the configuration pattern that is to be installed. Whilst the architecture of CHiP is very similar to that of later reconfigurable meshes, the programming model is quite different. In CHiP, a global controller changes a system wide interconnection pattern according to the actual processing phase. In contrast, reconfiguration in the reconfigurable mesh model is based on *connection autonomy*, that is, the processing elements independently decide, which pattern is to be installed at the locally connected switch elements.

Some of the authors of early reconfigurable mesh papers also published preliminary work on processor arrays that are enhanced with broadcasting resources. In [151], Stout proposes a mesh-connected computer with a unit-time global broadcasting support and shows that certain applications can profit from such capability. Prasanna-Kumar and Raghavendra extend the approach by a multiple broadcasting mechanism for array processors [89]. The presented architecture features broadcasting inside rows and columns of the array, which improves the runtime complexity for various problems compared to the global broadcast case.

First reconfigurable mesh inspired processor implementations, as the Polymorphic Processor Array, Content Addressable Array Parallel Processor, CLIP7A or Abacus (see Section 2.2.6 for details) were strictly SIMD based.

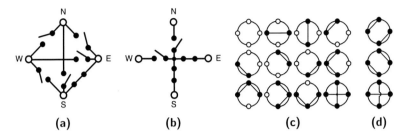

Figure 2.1: Switch element (SE) architecture and patterns: PARBS SE (a), RMESH SE (b), switch patterns supported by the RMESH model (c) and additional patterns which are supported by, e.g., the PARBS model (d).

That is, a single instruction is issued to all processing elements. Conditional statements were typically handled by consecutively processing the if part and else part of the condition and marking the actual active fraction of the processing elements by setting an *activity bit*. However, operating in SIMD mode is not obligatory for reconfigurable meshes by definition. More generally, the reconfigurable mesh can be associated to the Single Program Multiple Data (SPMD) model which allows multiple (and distinct) instruction streams to be executed concurrently.

2.2.2 Models

RMESH   Miller *et al.* were among the first who proposed an array of processors interconnected by a reconfigurable bus system [114]. They investigated an architecture, called reconfigurable mesh or RMESH, as well as basic algorithms for data movement, arithmetic, graph and image computations [113]. In the domain of reconfigurable meshes, the RMESH turned out to be the prevalent model. The RMESH architecture connects $N \times N$ PE in a 2-dimensional grid by reconfigurable buses. Each processor is connected to a local SE that itself is connected to the SEs of the north, east, west and south neighbors of the PE. A sketch of an RMESH SE is depicted in Figure 2.1(b). PEs can independently reconfigure their switches based on autonomous decisions. In the RMESH model, switches are allowed to either connect or disconnect from neighboring nodes. Hence, twelve so called connection patterns, shown in Figure 2.1(c), can be applied. One important consequence of this is that an RMESH PE is connected to at most one bus segment at any time. RMESH introduces the *unit-time* and the *log-time* broadcast delay model. The first model requires constant time broadcasts, the second one assumes that a communication phase may take $\log s$ steps, where s is the maximal number of SEs on a minimal path connecting two PEs on the same bus. In RMESH, communication follows the common write, concurrent read model. Buses are assumed to be $(\log N^2)$-bit wide, which allows to broadcast node IDs in a single communication step.

PARBS The Processor Array with Reconfigurable Bus System (PARBS) by Wang *et al.* [168] [169] [170] is the most general reconfigurable mesh model and embraces most model variations. PARBS meshes can be either two-dimensional or three-dimensional, having 4-port or 6-port switches, respectively. A PARBS switch for the two-dimensional case is shown in Figure 2.1(a). In contrast to RMESH, all possible fusing patterns for the switches are applicable resulting in 15 supported patterns for a two-dimensional mesh as depicted in Figure 2.1(c) and (d). PARBS assumes unit-time delay, word-level bus width and an exclusive write model.

Bit-Model While RMESH and PARBS operate on word-level data, Jang *et al.* [78] [80] introduce the bit-model of reconfigurable mesh. In this model, PEs have $\mathcal{O}(1)$ words of storage, words consists of $\mathcal{O}(1)$ bits and PEs can perform basic arithmetic and logic operations on $\mathcal{O}(1)$ bits of data in unit time. For the bit-model, number representation formats and conversions between several representations are of major importance [82]. As in PARBS, bit-model meshes can have 3-dimensional shape and any subset of the SEs' ports are allowed to get fused. In contrast to RMESH, model extensions like PARBS and the bit-model pose requirements on the system architecture that might, on the one hand, allow for the development of algorithms with outstanding runtime complexities, but on the other hand, make the models less implementable in practice.

Polymorphic Torus The peculiarity of the Polymorphic Torus model proposed by Li and Maresca [97] [96] are wraparound connections on each row and each column of the mesh. As the model allows for any possible fusing of its ports, it can be regarded as the most general two-dimensional PARBS variant. The Polymorphic Torus is of specific interest for this work as there exist a VLSI implementation as well as programming environment for the model (cf. 2.2.6).

RN   In order to achieve efficient self-simulation strategies (see Section 2.2.5), Ben-Asher *et al.* [25] identify restrictive reconfigurable mesh models which they call Reconfigurable Networks[1] (RN). One model restriction, named Horizontal-Vertical Reconfigurable Mesh (HV-RN), restricts the switches to only apply the $\{\mathtt{NS},\mathtt{W},\mathtt{E}\}$ and $\{\mathtt{WE},\mathtt{S},\mathtt{N}\}$ patterns and thus to form horizontal or vertical buses. The Linear Reconfigurable Mesh (LRN) allows the switches to fuse no more than two arbitrary ports, resulting in 10 possible connection patterns. In this case, only linear buses can be applied, which prevents split or merge operations at the switches. In contrast to RMESH, LRN supports the patterns $\{\mathtt{NE},\mathtt{SW}\}$, $\{\mathtt{NW},\mathtt{SE}\}$ and $\{\mathtt{NS},\mathtt{WE}\}$ which allow two buses traversing a single switch at a time. The General Reconfigurable Mesh (RN^2) supports any possible switch pattern and is in accordance with a two-dimensional PARBS model.

FR-Mesh   The Fusing Restricted reconfigurable mesh (FR-Mesh) allows only two of the 15 possible patterns, namely the *fusing* pattern $\{\mathtt{NEWS}\}$ and the *crossover* pattern $\{\mathtt{NS},\mathtt{EW}\}$ [61]. As a consequence, the authors can provide a self-simulation technique for this model that has limited simulation overhead.

k-constrained reconfigurable mesh   As a step into more practical models, Beresford-Smith *et al.* [29] propose the k-constrained reconfigurable mesh. This model restricts the maximal bus length to k. However, the authors show in [121] that if k is a constant, the k-constrained reconfigurable mesh is as powerful as the ordinary mesh and is not as powerful as the general reconfigurable mesh. To make the k-constrained reconfigurable mesh as powerful as the general reconfigurable mesh, k must be a function of the number of processors. This implies, though, that the maximal bus length is dependent on the algorithms' input size.

Directed Models   The directed reconfigurable network (DRN) is similar to the general reconfigurable mesh model, except that edges are directed. Consequently, messages can travel in one direction only and each edge splits into separate input and output edges. DRN can simulate any configuration of the general reconfigurable mesh in a single step, and thus, any algorithm developed for the undirected model can directly be applied to the directed

---

[1]   The terms reconfigurable network and reconfigurable mesh denote the very same principle, though the latter one has become established as the prevalent term. In this thesis, the original names of the model variations of the primal papers are used.

[2]   In a preliminary paper of Ben-Asher *et al.* the LRN model was established as the "Reconfigurable Network" [24].

model. In contrary, the undirected reconfigurable mesh can not simulate the directed model and, as a consequence, the directed reconfigurable mesh is the more powerful model. For a more detailed analysis of reconfigurable meshes concerning theoretical complexity aspects I refer to [26] and [27]. Another advantage of directed links lies in the increased bandwidth. Some algorithms profit from the doubled number of wires by overlapping several communication steps. This benefit does not influence the complexity class of an algorithm but can reduce the number of broadcasting steps by 50%.

Optical Models and Spin-Waves Additionally, optical models of the reconfigurable mesh, like the Array with Reconfigurable Optical Buses (AROB) by Pavel and Akl [138], the Linear Array with a Reconfigurable Pipelined Bus (LARPBS) by Pan and Hamdi [132] and the Optical Transpose Interconnection System (OTIS) by Marsden *et al.* [107] were studied. Recently, Yu *et al.* demonstrated a 3.125Gbps data transmission through a 4×4 multi-chip optical reconfigurable mesh [187]. Other authors explore unconventional communication channels. Eshaghian-Wilner *et al.* [55] [56] [58] present a nano-scale reconfigurable mesh that is interconnected with ferromagnetic spin-wave buses. As it is possible to simultaneously transmit multiple waves on each of the spin-wave sub-buses, the architecture allows for designing very fast and fault-tolerant algorithms. Using ferromagnetic spin-wave channels, waves instead of charge are transmitted on the buses and thus, the power consumption is presumably kept low. The related work in interconnects based on optical and nano technology shows that the reconfigurable mesh model, albeit developed as a model for VLSI, might suit the requirements of emerging technology very well.

2.2.3 Algorithms

Researchers have developed a vast amount of algorithms for the various reconfigurable mesh models. Two introductory examples shall point out how communication through a reconfigurable bus system can replace and speed-up traditional computation. The first algorithm computes the EXOR function over a sequence of N bits on a $3 \times 2N$ PARBS. Each input bit is distributed over separate contiguous blocks of 3×2 nodes. Depending on whether the local bit is '0' or '1', the sub-mesh installs the pattern depicted in Figure 2.2(a) or 2.2(b), respectively. For the actual computation, a signal is broadcast on the west port of the node in the top right corner of the mesh. If the signal exits the array on the topmost row (as it is the case for the example in Figure 2.2(c)) the result of the EXOR function is '0'. Otherwise, the signal

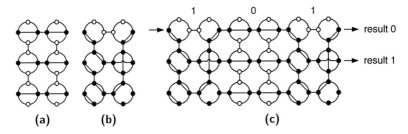

Figure 2.2: Exclusive OR PARBS algorithm: Block pattern for 0-bits (a) and 1-bits (b). Example for the function $1 \oplus 0 \oplus 1$ (c).

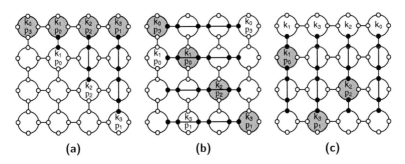

Figure 2.3: HV-RN permutation routing. Gray nodes indicate senders, other labeled nodes indicate destination PEs. Step 1: Broadcasting values to diagonal nodes (a). Step 2: Routing values to destination columns (b). Step 3: Routing values to topmost row (c).

flow ends in the second row of the array which indicates that the result of the EXOR function is '1'.

As a second example, I present permutation routing, a typical data movement operation for word-level reconfigurable meshes. An HV-RM is sufficient for the algorithm. However, as the HV-RM is a very restrictive model, it is also applicable to more universal models like RMESH or PARBS.

Permutation routing reorders a set of N objects (or values) according to a bijective function $\pi : \{0, 1, \ldots, N - 1\} \rightarrow \{0, 1, \ldots, N - 1\}$. The algorithm uses a mesh of size N^2 to permute N values. Figure 2.3 shows an example of permutation routing of four values $k_0 \ldots k_3$. Numbers p_y indicate that the

Problem	Mesh Size
EXOR of n bits	$3 \times 2n$
Permutation routing of n numbers	$n \times n$
Prefix-And of n 1-bit numbers	$1 \times n$
Maximum (minimum) of n $(\log n)$-bit numbers	$n \times n$
Addition of n k-bit numbers, $1 \leq k \leq n$	$n \times nk$
Multiplication of two n-bit numbers	$n \times n$
Division of two n-bit numbers	$n \times n$
Sort of n $\mathcal{O}(\log n)$ bit numbers	$n \times n$
Convex hull of n points	$n \times n$
Smallest enclosing rectangle of n points	$n \times n$
Triangulation of n planar points	$n^2 \times n$
All-pairs nearest neighbors of n points	$n \times n$
Two-set dominance counting of n points	$n \times n$

Table 2.1: Selected constant runtime algorithms for the reconfigurable mesh [33].

local value should be routed to position y. In a first step (see Figure 2.3(a)), the numbers k_x and p_y are moved to the diagonal of the mesh. Next, the k_x and p_y values are broadcast by the diagonal nodes on row buses (see Figure 2.3(b)). All nodes $P_{i,j}$ check whether the value k_x is dedicated to their local column, i.e., test if $y = j$. If the test fails, the node reconfigures the switch to set up the $\{\text{NS}, \text{E}, \text{W}\}$ pattern. Otherwise, the node disconnects the bus and broadcasts the value k_x on its N port. Finally, the nodes of the top row read the bus to receive their final value (see Figure 2.3(c)).

Referring to [33], Table 2.1 summarizes some other results for reconfigurable mesh algorithms. All of the listed examples have a runtime complexity of $\mathcal{O}(1)$. As they are of different complexity classes, the requirements regarding the numbers of PEs to solve the problem varies. In the remainder of this section, I summarize some reconfigurable mesh algorithm results for the application classes *Arithmetic*, *Sorting and Selection*, *Image Processing* and *Graph Algorithms*.

Arithmetic   Many basic arithmetic algorithms for the RMESH model are presented by Miller *et al.* [113]. Finding the maximum (minimum) of N values on $N \times N$ RMESH needs $\Theta(1)$ steps for the unit-time delay model and $\Theta(\log N)$ steps for the log-time delay model. Computing a logical OR (AND) function of N bits can be done on an RMESH of N processors in $\Theta(1)$ steps or in $\Theta(\log N)$ steps using the log-time delay model. N bits can be counted in constant time on a PARBS of size $(N + 1) \times N$ [171]. As an extension of bit counting, Olariu *et al.* present a method for modulo m counting N bits on a PARBS of size $(m+1) \times 2N$ [128]. Since the EXOR of N bits is equal to the modulo 2 sum of the bits, a $3 \times 2N$ PARBS can compute the EXOR of N bits in constant time (see Figure 2.2). As a consequence of this result, the authors conclude that the PARBS is "more powerful" than a CRCW PRAM, which requires $\Omega(\log N / \log \log N)$ time to compute the XOR of N bits [22]. Jang *et al.* developed an algorithm for adding N k-bit numbers given in BIN representation in $\mathcal{O}(1)$ time on an $N \times kN$ PARBS [81]. For a summary on results of addition algorithms see [159], pages 149–151. A constant time algorithm for multiplying two N-bit binary numbers on an $N \times N$ bit-model reconfigurable mesh is constructed by Jang *et al.* [136]. This result is optimal concerning the area-time (AT^2) complexity of VLSI for binary multiplication [38]. Park *et al.* present an optimal algorithm for integer division of two N-bit numbers on an $N \times N$ bit-level reconfigurable mesh in constant time [136]. In [160], Vaidyanathan *et al.* present various matrix-vector multiplication algorithms for the PARBS model. Middendorf *et al.* developed algorithms for multiplying several types of sparse $N \times N$ matrices on an $N \times N$ RMESH [112]. For the algorithms, also the LRN model would be sufficient, as the SEs have to fuse at most two ports at a time. In [135], Park *et al.* presented an AT^2 optimal matrix multiplication algorithm. Trahan *et al.* investigate arithmetical RMESH algorithms for floating point numbers, including addition and matrix vector multiplication [158].

Sorting and Selection   Lower bounds for parallel sorting are presented and discussed in [94] and [17]. In [154], Thompson and Kung developed an algorithm for sorting N numbers on an $N^{1/2} \times N^{1/2}$ regular mesh in $\Theta\left(N^{1/2}\right)$ time. Further mesh algorithms with same complexity come from Nassimi and Sahni [125] and Schnorr and Shamir [143]. Results for general meshes can in any way be applied to reconfigurable mesh models as they can simulate general meshes without overhead. An optimal algorithm for sorting N numbers in constant time on an $N \times N$ PARBS comes from Jang and Prasanna [82]. Similar results are provided by Lin *et al.* [100], Nigamand Sahni [126] and Olariu and Schwing [127].

Selection is the problem of finding the k-th smallest element in a totally ordered (but unsorted) set. Clearly, selection is no more complex than sorting, as it takes constant time to select the k-th smallest element out of a sorted set. A $\Theta(\log N)$ selection algorithm for N numbers on a reconfigurable mesh of N processors comes from Hao *et al.* [72]. It assumes at most N values distributed on a reconfigurable mesh with N processors. The Hao *et al.* algorithm improves the method of ElGindy and Wegrowicz, which needs $\Theta(\log^2 N)$ time [51].

Image Processing Miller *et al.* present a method for determining connected components on RMESH [113]. An algorithm for computing a histogram on PARBS is developed by Jang *et al.* [81]. Olariu *et al.* [130] present a constant time algorithm for computing the convex hull of N points on $N \times N$ LRN. Jang *et al.* [79] investigated a convex hull algorithm with same time complexity and mesh size for the PARBS model. Other contributions of the paper are algorithms for following related problems: smallest enclosing box, triangulation, all-pairs nearest neighbor, two-set dominance counting and three-dimensional maxima. Bokka *et al.* developed several constant time LRN algorithms for the following problems on convex polygons [31]: Convexity inclusion, supporting lines, stabbing, minimal area corner triangle, k-maximal element, intersection common tangent, private point and minimal distance. Voronoi diagram algorithms come from ElGindy and Wetherall [49] [50].

Graph Algorithms and Embeddings Wang and Chen introduce two $\mathcal{O}(1)$ algorithms for computing the transitive closure on PARBS [168]. The first algorithm is designed for a 3-dimensional PARBS of $N \times N \times N$, the second one for a 2-dimensional PARBS of $N^2 \times N^2$ processors. In both alternatives, N represents the number of vertices in the graph. Additionally, Wang and Chen provide various related graph algorithms for PARBS, e.g., connected component, articulation point, biconnected component, bridge, sorting, minimum spanning tree, multiplication of boolean matrices and bipartite graph recognition.

Miller *et al.* present a method for embedding graphs into reconfigurable meshes and show how the mesh-of-tree (with $3N - 2\sqrt{N}$ nodes) and the pyramid (with $\frac{4}{3}N - \frac{1}{3}$ nodes) architectures can be embedded into the RMESH (with N nodes). The overhead (see Section 2.2.5 for a definition of simulation overhead) for the simulation of algorithms is $\mathcal{O}(\log N)$ for the mesh-of-trees and $\mathcal{O}(1)$ for the pyramid architecture.

Model	#Nodes	#Links	Diameter	Avg. Dist.	Bisection	Degree
1D mesh (linear array)	k	$k-1$	$k-1$	$k/3$	1	2
1D torus (ring)	k	k	$k/2$	$k/4$	2	2
2D mesh (k-ary 2-mesh)	k^2	$2k(k-1)$	$2k-1$	$4k/3$	k	4
2D torus (k-ary 2-cube)	k^2	$2k^2$	k	$k/2$	$2k$	4
2D RMESH	k^2	$2k(k-1)$	1	NA	k	4
2D Polymorphic Torus	k^2	$2k^2$	1	NA	$2k$	4

Table 2.2: Topological parameters of some interconnect architectures.

2.2.4 Power of the Reconfigurable Mesh

The theoretical strength of the reconfigurable mesh model bases on its constant communication diameter which is due to the unit-time delay broadcast assumption. The diameter of a network is the maximum number of links that must be traversed to send a message to any node along a shortest path. In comparison to the reconfigurable mesh, general meshes (of size $k \times k$) have a diameter of $2k - 1$. Both, the general as well as the reconfigurable mesh have bisection width of k. The bisection width denotes the minimal number of edges that must be removed from a communication graph to split the graph in two subgraphs with identical (within one) number of vertices. As it is an important criterion for communication topologies, the bisection width is often applied to determine lower bounds, e.g., a low bisection width is an indicator of a communication bottleneck. If wraparound connections are added, mesh based topologies can increase their bisection width by a factor of d where d is the dimension of the mesh. Table 2.2 shows some topological parameters for the reconfigurable mesh and related interconnect architectures.

To relate the power of reconfigurable meshes to other parallel models, it is typically compared to the Parallel Random-Access Machine (PRAM) [63]. The PRAM is an idealized abstract model for a shared memory machine. It connects an arbitrary number of synchronous processors to an arbitrary size shared memory and allows constant time memory accesses. Depending on how parallel write accesses are resolved, one distincts *Concurrent Read Exclusive Write* (CREW) and *Concurrent Read Concurrent Write* (CRCW) PRAMs.

Although the PRAM is a very idealizing model of parallel computation, it is proven that any CRCW PRAM algorithm using N processors and S memory cells can be simulated by a HV-RN of size $N \times S$ in constant time [169]. With this result, Wang and Chen also provide a method for how to transform a PRAM algorithm to a reconfigurable mesh algorithm. Czumaj *et al.* [43] significantly improve the results by presenting a randomized N-processor CRCW PRAM simulation on an $N \times N$ reconfigurable mesh which guarantees constant delay for each simulated PRAM step. As the reconfigurable mesh is at least as powerful as the PRAM, it is sufficient to show that a single problem can be solved faster in order to prove that the reconfigurable mesh is the even "more powerful" model. Olariu *et al.* [128] and Miller *et al.* [113] present several $\mathcal{O}(1)$ algorithms for problems (including EXOR and parity computation for N bits) for which PRAM solutions require $\Omega(\log N / \log \log N)$ time.

Many more interesting results exist for the reconfigurable mesh. As an example, any problem that could be solved in $\mathcal{O}(\log N)$ time using polynomial size circuits[3], can be computed in constant time on an $N \times poly(N)$ LRN. Similar properties can be shown among reconfigurable mesh and Turing Machine models. For further reading, I refer to [24], [26] and, for broader information, to [159].

2.2.5 Self-Simulations

One practical shortcoming of reconfigurable mesh algorithms is the dependency of model and problem size. For instance, algorithms claim N or N^2 processors to solve problems of size N. Assuming many-core architectures of fixed size, techniques that allow to scale a reconfigurable mesh algorithm with problem size are of considerable interest. In literature, such techniques have been proposed and denoted as *self-* or *scaling-simulation*.

Self-simulation denotes the ability to simulate any algorithm for a certain reconfigurable mesh model on a different size instance of the same model. Thus, a self-simulation strategy is a general method to simulate step-by-step any algorithm for a specific reconfigurable mesh model. In [61], Fernandez-Zepeda *et al.* classify self-simulation techniques according to the *simulation overhead* f. Their definition is as follows:

For any $P < N$, let $\mathcal{M}(P)$ simulate a step of $\mathcal{M}(N)$ in $O\left(\frac{N}{P}f(N,P)\right)$ time. Then, the following holds true:

1. Model $\mathcal{M}$ has an optimal self-simulation if $f(N,P) = O(1)$.

2. Model $\mathcal{M}$ has a strong self-simulation if $f(N,P) = o(P)$.

---

[3] This set of problems is also denoted as complexity class NC^1.

3. Model $\mathcal{M}$ has a weak self-simulation if it does not have an optimal or strong scaling simulation.

The first term of the slowdown function, $\frac{N}{P}$, simply denotes the number of nodes that a single processor of the simulating mesh has to simulate. The simulation overhead f specifies the time complexity of simulating a single step of a single node of the original mesh. If a processor is able to simulate a step in constant time, that is, the time is neither dependent on the simulating mesh's size P nor on the simulated mesh's size N, the simulation is called optimal. If the simulation step is only dependent on the size of the simulating mesh P, the simulation strategy is called strong. If the simulation time is also dependent on the original mesh's size, it is called weak.

Processor Mappings A basic step of a self-simulation technique is to assign a set of logical PEs of the mesh that is to be simulated to physical PEs of the simulating mesh. Let a mesh $S = [0 : P - 1, 0 : Q - 1]$ of $P \times Q$ nodes simulate a larger mesh $R = [0 : N - 1, 0 : M - 1]$ of the same model. For ease of exposition, $\frac{N}{P}$ and $\frac{M}{Q}$ are assumed to be integers. The processor mappings are defined as follows:

- *Contraction mapping:* A contiguous region of the simulated mesh is mapped to a PE of the simulating mesh, i.e., $S(i,j)$ simulates
  $$R\left[i\frac{N}{P} : (i+1)\frac{N}{P} - 1, j\frac{M}{Q} : (j+1)\frac{M}{Q} - 1\right].$$

- *Window mapping:* A window of size $P \times Q$ is virtually shifted over the simulated mesh, i.e., $R(i,j)$ is simulated by processor $S(i \mod \frac{N}{P}, j \mod \frac{M}{Q})$.

- *Folded window mapping:* Windows of size $P \times Q$ are virtually folded up, i.e., $R(i,j)$ is simulated by $S(\mathit{fold}(i,P), \mathit{fold}(j,Q))$, where
  $$\mathit{fold}(a,b) = \begin{cases} a \mod b & \text{if } \lfloor \frac{a}{b} \rfloor \text{ is even} \\ b - 1 - (a \mod b) & \text{otherwise} \end{cases}$$

  This mapping technique is similar to window mapping but preserves more locality since some neighboring nodes of two windows are simulated by the same physical PE.

Figure 2.4 states examples for the three major processor mappings. In all cases, a 6×9 reconfigurable mesh is simulated by a 3×3 instance; the numbers in the figure denote the simulating processors.

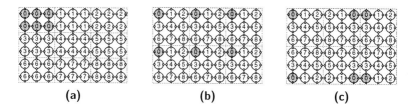

Figure 2.4: Mapping techniques for self-simulation [61]: contraction mapping (a), window mapping (b) and folded window mapping (c).

Self-Simulation Strategies Maresca proposes *virtual parallelism*[4] for a HV-RN implementation [102]. Ben-Asher *et al.* establish self-simulation techniques for the HV-RN, LRN and PARBS model [24]. The authors utilize three mapping techniques:

1. Contraction mapping allows optimal self-simulation for HV-RN. The authors prove that contraction mapping can not be used to optimally simulate LRN or even more powerful reconfigurable mesh models (RMESH, PARBS). More in detail, the lower bound for simulating a single step of an $N \times N$ algorithm on a $P \times P$ LRN is $\Omega(N)$ for every $P < N$.

2. Window mapping is used by an optimal LRN self-simulation.

3. Folded window mapping is the basis of an non-optimal self-simulation algorithm for the PARBS model.

Further results on self-simulation methods are given in [62], [109], and [120].

In the following, the HV-RN self-simulation technique of Ben-Asher *et al.* is outlined, because this method is most relevant for practical implementation. Switches can only be configured to form vertical or horizontal buses in the HV-RN model. Given this restriction, HV-RN simulation requires the following three steps:

1. Local (computation): Each PE in S simulates a $\frac{N}{P} \times \frac{M}{Q}$ sub-mesh of R, consisting of $k = \frac{NM}{PQ}$ cores, according to the contraction mapping technique. This can be done by linearizing the sub-mesh in row-major or column-major order. Let us assume row-major order where the rows of the sub-mesh are considered first, followed by the columns. In

---

[4] Originally, Maresca investigates an implementation of the reconfigurable mesh model as a restriction of the polymorphic torus. Later, Ben-Asher *et al.* coined the term LRN for a very similar model.

each row, the propagation of bus data is simulated from left to right and, subsequently, from right to left. Then, columns are considered and the propagation of bus data is simulated from top to bottom and, subsequently, from bottom to top. After these steps, each node has received the actual bus data, depending on whether it was a reader, a writer, or not using the bus at all. For the boundary nodes of the simulated sub-mesh, it has to be checked additionally whether they connect to sub-meshes simulated by other physical processors and, if so, whether there was a writer on the internal sub-bus and the data written. Overall, this phase takes $4k$ time steps.

Figure 2.5 shows an example where a physical processor $S(i, j)$ simulates a sub-mesh of 2×3 logical processors. The simulated sub-mesh with its concrete connection patterns is depicted in 2.5a). Figure 2.5b) presents the simulation of the communication in row-major order. The 2×3 boxes represent the data that is broadcast by the corresponding nodes of R; $\emptyset$ denotes that the corresponding processor does not write the bus. Starting from an initial state, data is propagated in the rows left to right and right to left. Then, the process is repeated on the columns. At the end, each node in R knows which data is present on its bus segment. During the simulation of the communication, the connections to other sub-meshes are analyzed. In the example, there is only one bus formed by the first column which is routed through the sub-mesh. Thus, when the physical processor $S(i, j)$ simulates the rows of the sub-mesh during the global communication phase, it will apply the $\{N, E, W, S\}$ pattern. When it simulates the columns, the pattern $\{NS, W, E\}$ will be applied for the first column and, again, $\{N, E, W, S\}$ for columns two and three. Figure 2.5c) summarizes the patterns and bus data used by $S(i, j)$ in the global communication phase.

2. Global (communication): In the second phase, the simulation algorithm considers all possible row and column buses that the nodes in S can be involved in. For a row u, assume a sequence of processors

$$R_L(u, v-1), R_C(u, v), \ldots, R_C(u, v + \frac{M}{Q} - 1), R_R(u, v + \frac{M}{Q}),$$

where nodes $R(i, j)$ are simulated by $S(\lfloor \frac{iP}{N} \rfloor, \lfloor \frac{iQ}{M} \rfloor)$, such that all nodes R_C are simulated by the same processor in S. Now consider two cases:

a) $R_L(u, v-1)$ and $R_R(u, v + \frac{M}{Q})$ belong to the the same bus. In this case, processor $S(\lfloor \frac{uP}{N} \rfloor, \lfloor \frac{vQ}{M} \rfloor)$ applies the $\{N, S, WE\}$ pattern and writes data onto the bus or not, depending on the collected information about $R_C(u, i)$.

b) $R_L(u, v-1)$ and $R_R(u, v + \frac{M}{Q})$ take part in different buses. In this case, processor $S(\lfloor \frac{uP}{N} \rfloor, \lfloor \frac{vQ}{M} \rfloor)$ applies the $\{\texttt{N}, \texttt{S}, \texttt{W}, \texttt{E}\}$ pattern and writes to its left neighbor depending on the collected information about $R_C(u, v)$ and to the right neighbor depending on the collected information about node $R_C(u, v + \frac{M}{Q} - 1)$.

The global communication phase consumes $2\frac{N}{P}$ steps for the horizontal buses. Additionally, $2\frac{M}{Q}$ steps are consumed for the vertical buses.

3. Finally, bus information must be updated for all simulated nodes that take part in buses and cross submesh borders. This can be done in $4k$ steps by linearization, similar to step 1.

The described HV-RN self simulation technique is called optimal because the simulation slowdown is ck, where $k = \frac{NM}{PQ}$ is the number of processors in R that are simulated by a single processor in S. Generally, a slowdown of k is unavoidable as the simulating mesh comprises k times less processors than the simulated mesh. The constant c is due to the additional cost of data transportation among the simulated nodes. For an exemplary implementation of the HV-RN self simulation technique see A.4, a detailed analysis of the runtime complexity for a specific reconfigurable mesh many-core is presented in Section 5.3.

When the underlying reconfigurable mesh model is less restrictive (than the HV-RN model), self-simulation techniques get more involved. One example is the LRN model which constrains the switches to only form linear buses, thus communication patterns that fuse more than three ports are not applicable. It has been shown that an optimal simulation of the LRN model is not achievable by methods that base on a contraction mapping [23]. However, the window mapping permits an optimal simulation of $N \times N$ meshes by $P \times P$ meshes for the linear model. As the detailed algorithm is quite complex, I only present the essential aspects here.

The algorithm proceeds in two phases: A forward phase scans the folded mapped windows of the simulated mesh in a snake like manner. If a bus segment is completely embedded in the current window, the algorithm step can be computed in an unmodified way. If the bus segment crosses window boundaries it is assigned an ID, data and start point information. Boundary nodes of the window are responsible for storing this information. Here, the folded window property is beneficial, because neighboring boundary nodes are simulated by the same processors. However, bus segments can take a winding curve through multiple windows. For this reason, several advanced techniques are used to preserve optimality of the simulation. The backward phase examines the windows in the opposite direction of the previous phase

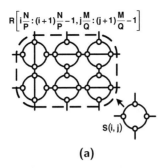

(a)

Simulation	Pattern($S(i,j)$)	Bus($S(i,j)$)
Row #1	$\{\texttt{N},\texttt{E},\texttt{W},\texttt{S}\}$	$\texttt{W}:\emptyset$ $\texttt{E}:3$
Row #2	$\{\texttt{N},\texttt{E},\texttt{W},\texttt{S}\}$	$\texttt{W}:\emptyset$ $\texttt{E}:5$
Column #1	$\{\texttt{NS},\texttt{E},\texttt{W}\}$	$\texttt{NS}:4$
Column #2	$\{\texttt{N},\texttt{E},\texttt{W},\texttt{S}\}$	$\texttt{N}:\emptyset$ $\texttt{S}:\emptyset$
Column #3	$\{\texttt{N},\texttt{E},\texttt{W},\texttt{S}\}$	$\texttt{N}:\emptyset$ $\texttt{S}:\emptyset$

(c)

$\emptyset$	$\emptyset$	3
4	5	$\emptyset$

Initial state

$\emptyset$	$\emptyset$	3
4	5	5

Rows:
left to right

$\emptyset$	3	3
4	5	5

Rows:
right to left

$\emptyset$	3	3
4	5	5

Columns:
top-down

4	3	3
4	5	5

Columns:
bottom-up

(b)

Figure 2.5: Illustration of one step of the HV-RN self-simulation algorithm. (a) Node $S(i,j)$ simulates the sub-mesh $R\left[i\frac{N}{P} : (i+1)\frac{N}{P} - 1, j\frac{M}{Q} : (j+1)\frac{M}{Q} - 1\right]$. (b) Simulate communication in local sub-mesh. (c) Parameters for simulating global communication (Phase 2).

to deliver data to the reading processors. Both phases cause a constant time overhead for simulating a single window. Overall, this algorithm leads to an optimal slowdown factor of $\Theta\left(\frac{N^2}{P^2}\right)$.

For the simulation of an $N \times N$ mesh by a mesh with $P \times P$ processors in the general reconfigurable mesh model, no optimal solution is known.

A rather sophisticated technique given in [25] comes with a slowdown of $\mathcal{O}\left(\frac{N^2}{P^2}\log N \log \frac{N}{P}\right)$. The simulation algorithm uses $\mathcal{O}\left(\frac{N^2}{P^2}\right)$ extra space for temporary storage at each processor of the $N \times N$ mesh.

2.2.6 Reconfigurable Mesh Implementations

Maresca was one of the first who addressed practicability aspects and the lack of a programming model for the reconfigurable mesh [102]. The Polymorphic Processor Array (PPA) is among the few implementations incorporating reconfigurable mesh principles [102]. It is based on a horizontal-vertical reconfigurable mesh (HV-RN) with wraparound connections and directed links. Thus, a SE always has one incoming and one outgoing port. Unlike HV-RN, all switches of the PPA are configured to the same global connection pattern at a time. Further, the switches are either in the OPEN or the SHORT state. In the SHORT state, the two ports of a switch are fused according to the global communication pattern. In the OPEN state, the bus is split at the incoming port of the local SE. PPA uses a strict SIMD programming model, where all processors execute exactly the same instruction. Corresponding to the architecture, Maresca also introduced a new language called Polymorphic Parallel C (PPC) [103]. In PPC, data objects can be either scalar or parallel. Scalar objects are associated to a central controller, whereas parallel objects are individually kept in local memory by each PE. PPA is a very restrictive variant of the reconfigurable mesh model, limited to only a subset of the entire body of reconfigurable mesh algorithms. To evaluate the cost of the polymorphic-torus interconnection in term of VLSI area, a VLSI chip called YUPPIE (Yorktown ultra-parallel polymorphic image engine) [104] has been designed. The chip contains 16 processors, each of which is equipped with a one-bit ALU, five registers, and 256 bit memory. The chip is designed with a $2\mu m$ CMOS technology. The authors show that additional reconfigurable mesh related functionality costs only 20% of the silicon area, but can deliver orders of magnitude of performance improvement over non-reconfigurable mesh networks.

CAAPP (Content Addressable Array Parallel Processor) [175] works with mesh of 1-bit PEs connected through the so-called coterie network[5] [148]. In contrast to YUPPIE, where the global instruction selects between one of two possible communication patterns, each PE of CAAPP autonomously

---

[5] The IUA system was developed in joint work by the Hughes Research Laboratories and the University of Massachusetts at Amherst. While the Amherst authors call the reconfigurable mesh like network *coterie network* the authors from Hughes prefer the name *Gated Connection Network* (GCN).

establishes the switch setting. A single CAAPP processor chip integrates 256 1-bit PEs and is applied at the lowest level of the hierarchical Image Understanding Architecture (IUA) [176]. The IUA is programmed in C++ by the use of a dedicated image processing class library.

Other massively parallel processors that focus on image algorithms are those of the CLIP series. The CLIP7A [65] extends former (pure SIMD) CLIP processors by incorporating more local control. Although it is arranged as a linear array, the CLIP7A processor can be considered as a reconfigurable mesh implementation because of its ability to reconfigure the interconnection network based on autonomous decisions. Programming of the CLIP7A is based on a microprogramming language called Mik. A prototype implementation of the CLIP7A processor consists of 256 16-bit PEs distributed over 128 processor cards, each of which implements 2 PEs.

In contrast to CLIP7A, the Abacus processor adheres to the concept of bit serial PEs [32]. The VLSI implementation of the Abacus array integrates 1024 elementary 1-bit PEs on a single die. A single PE can connect its output port to the output port of a selected neighboring PE via a wired OR. This feasibility makes the interconnection network of Abacus a reconfigurable mesh.

Several researchers developed simulators for the reconfigurable mesh, e.g., RMSIM [119], JRM [117], JRSim [152] and the simulator described in [150]. For the Polymorphic Processor Array and its programming language PPC, Maresca and Baglietto presented a corresponding simulator [103]. Along the same line, [18] reported on RPC++, a SIMD language and simulator for reconfigurable processor arrays. RPC++ extends the standard C language by several control structures and data types. For instance, variables can be declared to be *poly* which implies that each PE has its own copy of a value.

2.3 Circuit-Switched Interconnects for Many-Cores

Networks-on-chip (NoC) have become a generally accepted communication technology for future many-core systems [28] [30] [101]. Most current proposals advocate packed-switched NoCs and scale compute cluster infrastructures to a single chip [44]. While such approaches rely on well-understood communication architectures and widely-used message passing programming abstractions, they also consume substantial amounts of energy and silicon area. Packet-switched NoCs are known to be affected by a variety of design trade-offs, regarding energy dissipation, latency, throughput and area [133] [39]. A prime example is Intel's Terrascale project with the goal to minimize the energy consumption by restricting the on-chip network to consume only 10% of the overall power budget. However, recent implementations are still too power hungry, consuming significantly more than a quarter of the total energy [77].

In contrast to packet-switched NoCs, circuit-switched networks create end-to-end connections which are often established during run time. Subsequently, there is no need to buffer large amounts of data within the switches. For example, Wolkotte *et al.* [183] have found that circuit-switching entails a significant reduction in energy consumption. Although establishing a connection can lead to a high latency, the bandwidth provided by circuit-switched interconnects is generally high and predictable. Thus, Wiklund and Liu have demonstrated the benefits of circuit-switching for real-time applications, based on their SoCBUS architecture [179].

Still, both packet- and circuit-switched networks share the need for intelligent routers that make decisions on where to forward an incoming packet or connection, respectively. Such routers lead to a significant overhead in energy and area which is caused to a high degree by header analysis [20]. Packet-switched routers consume additional power for packet buffering. In their 2009 paper on *Outstanding Research Problems in NoC Design* [101], Marculescu *et al.* state: "In order for NoCs to be an efficient and effective replacement of dedicated wires as the primary communication fabric, there is a need for new switching techniques that can obviate this router overhead and truly deliver the energy-delay-throughput of dedicated wires." One alternative switching technique takes into account that many applications and programming models do not require dynamic routing decisions at all. The energy and latency overheads posed by dynamic routing can be avoided by a circuit-switched network controlled by pre-computed sequences of switch settings, so called *communication schedules*. There are a number of many-core projects utilizing exactly such an interconnect:

- *iWarp/NuMesh:* The iWarp architecture allows programs to access the communication infrastructure to implement systolic communication mechanisms [36, 68, 69]. In [147], Shoemaker et al. have expanded this concept to the NuMesh architecture. In NuMesh, each node in a regular 3D Mesh topology contains a communication finite state machine, which is a dedicated programmable controller that routes message traffic among neighboring nodes according to a pre-compiled pattern. As communication patterns are determined at compile time, the topology is arranged by programming rather than by dynamic routing.

- *aSoC:* The communication architecture of the adaptive system-on-a-chip (aSoC) is based on light-weight interfaces connecting heterogeneous elements like microprocessors, memories, ALUs and reconfigurable logic in a 2D mesh topology. aSoC aims at inter-core communication in form of data streams using statically computed communication schedules for each network interface. A dedicated application mapping tool flow extracts assembly code for processors as well as HDL code for the reconfigurable devices out of a C/C++ specification [99].

- *RAW:* The RAW microprocessor from MIT uses several overlaid networks for different purposes. While wormhole-routed networks are used for dynamic events, a lower latency static network is used for the register level transportation of single operands among processing tiles [153, 167]. The RAWCC compiler schedules send/receive instructions to the cores as well as to the switches [93].

- *Commercial Many-cores:* Recently, a number of commercial products have been presented using circuit-switched networks. Tilera's Tile64 [156] is based on the RAW project and integrates 64 32-bit three way VLIW cores. The interconnect comprises five mesh networks, one of which uses circuit-switching [178]. PicoChip [47, 134] attaches four PEs over a unidirectional bus system to a configurable switch. The buses use software-scheduled time-division multiplex which assigns logical connections to time slots at compile time. At run-time, the switches execute their local schedule without any need for arbitration. The PC102 chip comprises 322 PEs. MathStar [108] offers an array of so-called silicon objects which can be 16-bit ALUs, register files, multiply & accumulate units, and I/O units, programmed by an FPGA-like design flow. The communication infrastructure uses 21-bit buses organized into nearest neighbor links and party lines which are connections for bypassing nearest neighbors. A silicon object can read, forward and replace any input to any output party line. Element CXI [83] proposes an architecture comprised of 16-bit PEs, memory elements, and control elements. Four of these elements are grouped into a so-called zone and are connected via a crosspoint switch. Four zones form a cluster. The first production device contained four such clusters.

While the above-mentioned approaches extract the sequence of settings for each switch out of some specification during compile time, more radical approaches reconfigure the overall topology. It is known that the interconnect topology has a major impact on the performance of a parallel system [133, 141]. Going a step further, Vassiliadis and Sourdis argue that a system's demand concerning the network topology changes even during a single program run [163]. Hence, they propose to reconfigure the interconnect in response to algorithm requirements in a fine-grained, FPGA-like manner.

Another example for altering the topology is the work of Kissler et al. [85]. They propose a so-called weakly programmable processor array which connects application-specific PEs in a regular grid. The interconnection topology is dynamically reconfigurable as a whole, or for specific areas of the grid. Each PE stores an adjacency matrix that defines the connection pattern for the local switch.

2.4 Realizing Many-Cores on FPGAs

The experimental evaluation of novel approaches for future many-cores is a challenge of its own. Simulation will be by far too slow or inaccurate to cover reasonably complex systems, and prototype VLSI fabrication will be prohibitively expensive. Hence, researchers leverage reconfigurable hardware technology to emulate realistic many-cores. Such reconfigurable platforms and the required libraries of cores and network-on-chip components, often denoted as *gateware*, are currently being pushed as the new vehicle for future computer architecture research [16].

The most prominent example is the Research Accelerator for Multiple Processors project (RAMP), which is a collaboration of several working groups for building emulation engines for massively parallel system based on several communication models [173]. The RAMP project splits into several branches. While RAMP White investigates a cache coherent SoC [15], RAMP Red looks into transactional memory techniques [174], and RAMP Blue explores message passing communication infrastructures for future many-cores [88]. For example, a recent RAMP implementation integrates more than 1000 Xilinx Microblaze 32-Bit RISC soft cores on a multi-FPGA system. Recently, a fourth branch of the RAMP project (RAMP Gold) was formed to investigate an FPGA prototype for the UC Berkeley InfiniCore model.

Another project that is looking into message passing for FPGA-based architectures is the Toronto Molecular Dynamics machine [137] [140]. Here, the researchers investigate an MPI implementation for multi-FPGA systems with the goal to hide hardware complexity from the software programmer. Williams *et al.* [181] have presented a similar approach focusing on an array of Picoblaze processors attached to a Microblaze host for programming [180].

2.5 Chapter Summary and Conclusions

This chapter provides the background needed for the thesis. After a short classification of parallel programming models and implementations thereof, I present the reconfigurable mesh model in detail. At this point, the reader should be aware of how reconfigurable mesh algorithms work in principle and that there is a wide range of model variations. I present theoretical aspects of the reconfigurable mesh model as well as practical aspects like scaling simulations.

The last part of this chapter presents related work concerning circuit-switched interconnects for many-cores and selective projects that use FPGAs for many-core prototyping. In particular, I refer to some architectures which also rely on *scheduled communication*, a specific form of circuit-switching. This method, albeit used for different programming models, is related to the communication style of reconfigurable meshes.

The landscape of reconfigurable mesh research is characterized by a bulk of theory work and only few practical studies that build systems based on the model. The few reconfigurable mesh implementations were built in the early 90's, when the model became popular. However, in the last years, the model re-attracted interest as the switch elements suit the specific demands of emerging communication technologies like optical wave-guides or spin-waves.

CHAPTER 3

Architecture of Reconfigurable Mesh Many-Cores

This chapter presents the general architecture of reconfigurable mesh many-cores and the design of basic building blocks. At first, SEs and PEs are discussed, as both are inherent parts of a reconfigurable mesh. Afterwards, I introduce a control network that implements a barrier mechanism which can be used to control the lock-step execution of reconfigurable mesh algorithms. Finally, I summarize the area utilization and timing results of reconfigurable mesh many-cores implemented in FPGA technology.

3.1 Switch Elements

The SEs are tightly connected to and under full control of the PEs. In the RMESH model [113] that serves as inspiration for the interconnect, a PE can read and write from and to four ports, named N, E, S, and W, and control the setting of these ports. A PE can either disconnect its switch from the surrounding switches, or fuse two or more ports to connect itself to neighboring nodes. Driven by FPGA technology, the implementation presented in this thesis uses a directed network model. That is, the originally bidirectional links of the reconfigurable mesh model are replaced by directed ones and each of the ports N, E, S, and W splits into separated in ports and out ports, e.g., N_{in} and N_{out} for the N-Port. The directed reconfigurable mesh can simulate any configuration of the general reconfigurable mesh, and thus, any algorithm developed for the undirected model can directly be applied

0: {N,S,W,E}	4: {NE,S,W}	8: {NWE,S}	12: {N}
1: {NS,W,E}	5: {N,W,SE}	9: {NES,W}	13: {S}
2: {N,S,WE}	6: {N,E,SW}	10: {N,ESW}	14: {W}
3: {NW,S,E}	7: {NWS,E}	11: {NSWE}	15: {E}

Table 3.1: Coding of reconfigurable mesh patterns.

to the directed model. In contrary, the undirected reconfigurable mesh can not simulate the directed model and, as a consequence, the directed reconfigurable mesh is the more powerful model. For a more detailed analysis of reconfigurable meshes concerning theoretical complexity aspects I refer to [26]. Another advantage of directed links is that some algorithms profit from the doubled number of wires by overlapping several communication steps. This positive effect does not influence the complexity class of an algorithm, but can reduce the number of broadcasting steps by 50%.

The SE is implemented to be highly parameterizable, e.g., all the data links can be configured in their bit-width. Three alternative SE implementations are supported, providing a trade-off between design complexity and versatility with respect to the supported reconfigurable mesh model:

- The HV-RN SE can switch only the patterns {NS,E,W}, {N,S,EW} and {N,S,E,W}, and corresponds to the horizontal-vertical reconfigurable mesh model that forms row and column buses,

- the LRN SE implements the linear reconfigurable mesh model which allows to fuse any two ports of an SE (patterns 0–6 in Figure 2.1) and, finally

- the RMESH SE allows for all configuration patterns shown in Figure 2.1 and is the most general switch.

The designer can significantly reduce resource utilization and the switch's delay by restricting the set of supported switch patterns at compile time. A list of all possible switch patterns and corresponding IDs is depicted in Table 3.1.

Figure 3.1 shows the schematic of a part of the SE. The PE can write data to the switch through the P_{in} port, read data from the switch through the P_{out} port, and set the local connection pattern of the switch through the *sel* port. Figure 3.1 details the multiplexing for the outgoing north port N_{out} of the SE. Connection patterns joining several ports are realized over a wired OR.

Switches can also be configured to be purely combinational or buffered. The

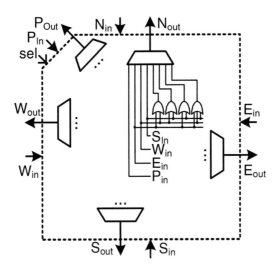

Figure 3.1: Schematic for the RMESH switch with detailed multiplexing for the outgoing north port.

unbuffered SE follows the actual semantics of the reconfigurable mesh. However, using a combinational switch can lengthen the critical path in an unacceptable manner. To overcome this issue, one can expand the communication phase to multiple clock cycles. This method is related to the k-constrained reconfigurable mesh [29] which restricts the maximal bus length to at most k switches. Expanding the communication phase to multiple cycles conceptually violates the reconfigurable mesh model's principles but is practically a very fast way of communicating operands.

Figure 3.1 shows an SE for a pure combinational network that has been studied in [2]. Unbuffered switches are difficult to handle with current FPGA design tools, because their support of multi-cycle paths comes with numerous limitations. To this end, the many-core prototypes presented in this thesis use a buffered counterpart which includes single word registers at the outgoing ports. When using buffered switches, path delays inside the mesh network become fairly short which allows for high clocking rates of the data network.

3.2 Processing Elements

3.2.1 Choice of Processing Elements

First reconfigurable mesh implementations like YUPPIE [105] or the Content Addressable Array Parallel Processor (CAAPP) of the Image Understanding Architecture [175] use large-scale meshes of simple 1-bit PEs. In contrast, my approach is to employ more complex PEs to advance the reconfigurable mesh to a realistic many-core model. In order to be able to employ different processors or implementations of algorithmic state machines as PEs, the interface to the reconfigurable mesh based network is kept plain. The processor has to provide a buffered output word to the network which is to be enhanced with a single bit indicating a valid data word. The bit-width of data words is made configurable. To install the switch configuration, the PE outputs the actual 4-bit configuration pattern to the SE.

In this thesis, I discuss two alternative PE implementations as representatives for different classes of reconfigurable mesh many-cores. First, a deterministic PE allows for the processor array to operate in a SIMD like fashion. If instruction execution of a PE is deterministic, the compiler can determine the execution time for program specifications – except for loops that are bounded by dynamic values – at compile time. By padding program paths, the compiler synchronizes the execution of a parallel application in a fine-grained manner. Although the multiple processors execute individual programs, the overall execution is kept synchronous. As a second PE, a 32-bit RISC core is used as a representative for a powerful embedded processor. Both PEs are based on soft CPUs which serve as the principal processing constituent of the core and are detailed in the following sections.

Architecture	PE	SE model	PEs/chip	Mesh size	Programming
Systolic/scheduled communication					
iWARP [139]	32-bit	Torus	1	1024	Apply [21]
NuMesh [147]	32-bit	Mesh	1[1]	NA	Comm. compiler
aSoc [99]	heterog.	Mesh	7×7[1]	NA	Mapping Tools
RAW [167]	32-bit	Mesh	16	4×4	e.g. RawCC [93]
Tilera [10]	32-bit	Mesh	100	10×10	C + Libraries
Picochip [134]	16-bit	Clustered Mesh	~300	NA	C/Assembler
CLIP4 [64]	1-bit	(Hexa) Mesh	8	96×96	Microcode
CLIP7A [65]	16-bit	Linear Array	2	1×256	Mik [110]
Reconfigurable mesh					
YUPPIE [104]	1-bit	Polym. Torus	4×4	4×4	PPC [103]
CAAPP [175]	1-bit	RMESH	8×8	512×512[176]	Custom Library
Abacus [32]	1-bit	RMESH[3]	16×64	16×64	SIMD style
This thesis					
Picoblaze Mesh	8-bit	RMESH	16×16	128×128[1]	ARMLang
Microblaze Mesh	32-bit	RMESH	6×6	8×8[4]	C

[1] Simulation only.
[2] Intended size. A 1/64th slice of the intended system was built as proof-of-concept
[3] Uses a restricted version of RMESH.
[4] Implemented on a single Virtex-4 LX200 device.

Table 3.2: Overview of reconfigurable mesh implementations and related architectures that use a systolic or scheduled communication style.

3.2.2 Picoblaze Processing Element

The Picoblaze is a very small footprint 8-bit microcontroller that comes with a fully predictable timing behavior as each instruction always consumes two clock cycles. It is intended for sequential control and simple data processing, e.g., to replace complex state machines implemented in FPGA logic. The Picoblaze version used in this thesis is the KCPSM3[1] (where PSM stands for "Programmable State Machine") which is optimized for the Spartan-3 family of Xilinx FPGAs [185].

The Picoblaze supports 16 byte-wide general-purpose data registers and a 64-byte internal scratchpad RAM. Up to 1024 instructions are stored in one 18k Block RAM memory of the FPGA. I/O is port-mapped, i.e., with every register INPUT or OUTPUT instruction, an 8-bit so called *port_id* supplies the port identifier or port address for the associated operation. If only a small number of IO channels have to be differentiated, one should use one-hot coding of port IDs to simplify decoding. On a Spartan-3 device, the Picoblaze core occupies 96 FPGA slices. The Picoblaze is programmed in a rather simple assembly language, for which an assembler tool is delivered together with the core. It should be noticed that there is no higher-level language compiler available for the Picoblaze[2].

Because of its characteristics, the Picoblaze is an ideal PE to study a large scale processor array on FPGA devices. Its very limited resource requirements allow for placing hundreds of individually programmable cores on a larger FPGA. As the Picoblaze specification is available as low-level Xilinx device specific VHDL code, it is possible to modify the core's design.

I/O Operations   To implement a proper interface to the SE, the Picoblaze is encapsulated into a wrapper module. The wrapper stores I/O data and controls the state of the Picoblaze. Every I/O operation is realized by an INPUT or OUTPUT instruction to a specific port_id.To reconfigure the SE, a Picoblaze outputs the actual switch pattern ID (*cf.* Table 3.1) to port_id 0. The wrapper stores this patterns and delivers it to the SE. A broadcast to the local bus segment is done by the operation OUTPUT sX, 02, where sX is the register to be written and 02 is the port_id. The wrapper buffers sX, enhances the 8-bit data word with a valid bit and forwards it to the

---

[1]   Recently (10/2010), a new Picoblaze version (KCPSM6) was announced, which is optimized for newer Xilinx devices. However, in the following the term "Picoblaze" denotes the KCPSM3 module.

[2]   In 2005 Francesco Poderico provided an initial approach of a Picoblaze C-compiler as Microsoft Windows binary. The tool was able to translate a subset of C statements to rather unoptimized assembly code. Currently, it is not available anywhere for download.

mesh network. Every data that is passing a switch is visible to the local PE through the P_{in} port. If the wrapper identifies valid data at its switch, it copies the word into a local buffer. Data obtained from the network is made accessible to the Picoblaze through port number 4. With INPUT sY, 04, the core reads the most recent data that passed the local SE into its register sY.

Controlling the Core's State For synchronization and power management purposes, it is beneficial to be able to stall the PE. An ideal method for freezing the state of a sequential circuit is clock gating. On FPGA technology, one can differentiate between two variants of clock gating. A dedicated signal, e.g., a stall signal, is used to either control the clock enable inputs of the flip-flops or to switch off certain parts of the built-in clock network. While the first approach can reduce the switching power inside the FPGA logic, the latter approach is also able to reduce the power caused by the clock network itself. Wang *et al.* have demonstrated in [172] that gating the clock tree leads to higher power savings than merely using the clock enable signals of the flip-flops. However, controlling the clock network is also less flexible due to the limited number of internal clock buffers. For example, Virtex-5 devices come with 32 global clock lines, each of which can be driven by one clock buffer. Due to this limitation, clock tree gating can not be used for the proposed reconfigurable mesh prototypes because each individual PE would require a separate clock line and the number of PEs easily extends the limit of 32.

The Picoblaze that I use as PE natively does not come with any stalling capabilities. Therefore, I modified the Picoblaze design to support a stall mode in which switching activity inside the processor is significantly reduced. In particular, the Picoblaze design is extended by an incoming stall signal which is used to disable the program counter and to prevent the registers from being written. This way, the switching activity is dramatically reduced and the core consumes just a fraction of its typical dynamic power.

The stalling mechanism is used for controlling two features: barrier synchronization and power management. When arriving at a barrier synchronization point in the program, a core issues an OUTPUT operation to port_id 32 that sends the core to the stalled mode. Additionally, the core issues a '1' signal on the global barrier net (c.f. Section 3.3). Figure 3.2(a) illustrates the state machine that controls this mechanism. When all cores have reached the barrier, a centralized controller broadcasts a signal to all PEs via a dedicated control net. When the PEs receive such signal, they release their stall signal and synchronously continue with program execution. The power management mechanism is completely software-driven and is presented in detail in Chapter 7.

The hardware realization of the low-power, or sleep mode is very similar to the barrier mode. During the execution of a parallel program, a core might decide to call an OUTPUT operation on port_id 64 in order to switch itself off. In that case, the Picoblaze gets immediately stalled, while the SE and the local network interface remain active. If one (or multiple) of the remaining active nodes execute a wakeup operation (OUTPUT to port_id 128), all nodes of the processor array are notified to continue. Being in sleep mode, a PE also issues a barrier signal because the active PEs could otherwise be waiting endlessly for a switched-off node. The sleep/wakeup mechanism, like the barrier synchronization mechanism of the reconfigurable mesh, works on global control signals. As the Picoblaze core itself is not able to operate when being stalled, the wrapper controls the barrier mechanism and the sleep mode.

3.2.3 Microblaze Processing Element

The Microblaze is a 32-bit embedded RISC processor soft core optimized for Xilinx FPGA devices [186]. In contrast to the Picoblaze core, its specification is not open-source so that it is not (reasonably) possible to modify the core. However, the Microblaze is highly configurable allowing the user to select from diverse features.

The Microblaze processor is implemented with a Harvard memory architecture and comes with 32 32-bit general purpose registers. The single issue pipeline can be configured to three or five stages. A variety of interfaces are supported by the core, including the AMBA Advanced eXtensible Interface 4 (AXI4), IBM CoreConnect On-chip Peripheral Bus (OPB), Xilinx Local Memory Bus (LMB), Xilinx Cache Link (XCL), and Xilinx Fast Simplex Link (FSL). Microblaze CPUs can be equipped with dedicated hardware multipliers and floating point coprocessors. A performance-optimized Microblaze can be clocked up to 307 MHz on a Virtex-6 device and reaches 1.19 Dhrystone MIPS per MHz.

I/O Operations Microblaze PEs use FSL interfaces for communication and switch reconfiguration. FSLs are FIFO based point-to-point communication channels which are accessible with a very low latency. The Microblaze ISA comprises put and get instructions which can be used to transfer data to and from the register file on the processor to hardware running on the FPGA. FSL connections are normally implemented as two uni-directional FIFO-based communication channels, data transfers to and from FSL FIFOs are typically completed in two clock cycles. FSL interfaces can be accessed in a blocking or non-blocking mode. Additionally, an FSL transfer can be marked with a *control* flag.

The Microblaze PEs use the FSL0 interface of the core to connect to both, an outgoing and an incoming FIFO. Blocking put and get instructions access this interface and implement 32-bit broadcasts to the local bus segment and read operations from the local bus segment, respectively. A core gets stalled during a write operation when the outgoing FIFO is full and during a read operation as long there is no data present in the incoming FIFO. The FSL0 interface also handles the reconfiguration of the SE. In contrast to a general put operation which causes a broadcast to the bus segment, a reconfiguration put is marked with a control flag. The network interface controller (NIC) interprets data labeled with such a control flag as a switch pattern and sets its configuration register accordingly.

As for the Picoblaze PEs, the Microblaze interface to the reconfigurable mesh network forwards every valid data word to the processor that passes the switch. Valid data is labeled by a valid bit and is pushed into the FIFO of the FSL0 link when detected. The processors access the data by calling get instructions on the FSL0 link.

In contrast to the Picoblaze reconfigurable mesh FPGA implementation, the interconnect of the Microblaze based implementation allows bus writers to broadcast sequences of data words onto their local bus segments. Broadcasting multiple words is beneficial as it can significantly reduce the number of synchronized communication phases if the algorithm includes the transmission of larger bunches of data. However, when using this efficient multi-word broadcasts, the programmer either has to take care of cyclic sub-buses inside the mesh or use algorithms that avoid them altogether. For example, assume a mesh network where every switch is configured into the {NEWS} pattern. A broadcast of one node would be duplicated three times at every switch and the incoming FIFOs of the PEs would get flooded by redundant data. If a broadcast is limited to a single word, message duplication is not a problem since the single word message buffer will anyway be rewritten with the same value. Furthermore, one can disable the SE for the rest of the communication phase if valid data has already been routed through.

A second FSL interface of the Microblaze PEs is used to connect to the barrier network (c.f. Section 3.3). The sync command consists of two subsequent FSL-instructions. First an fslput instruction causes the barrier core to issue a '1' signal on the barrier net. This instruction is always followed by an blocking fslget. As the barrier core normally denotes to the incoming FSL port of the Microblaze that no data is available, the get instruction is blocked and the core gets stalled automatically. If the barrier net broadcasts a continuation signal, the barrier core reports valid data at the incoming FIFO of the Microblaze. As a result, the get instruction can run to completion and the cores step into the next program phase.

Controlling the Cores' State Unlike the Picoblaze, the Microblaze processor supports a built-in stall mechanism. That means, when executing a blocking FSL put or get, the core automatically gets stalled if the FIFO operation can not be executed immediately. This property can be used to implement an implicit synchronization of the reconfigurable mesh communication phases if the following requirements are fulfilled: i) every sub-bus has exactly one bus-writer, ii) nodes, which are no writers are readers and consume as many words as the sub-bus writer broadcasts onto the bus segment, and iii) processors must not reconfigure the switches until the current communication phase has finished. This restriction is essentially not a serious limitation, because most reconfigurable mesh algorithms naturally operate in this style or can be transformed to fulfill principles i)–iii).

3.3 Control Networks

The many-core prototypes implement a barrier network through a high-speed wired-AND. The FPGA realization of the wired-AND builds on the carry chains and is shown in Figure 3.2(b). All nodes on a single column of an $N \times N$ reconfigurable mesh stick to the same carry chain. The sync-signal $P(k)_{sync}$ is used as select for a carry chain multiplexer ($MUXCY$). If a node k ($0 \leq k < N$) sets $P(k)_{sync} = 1$, the incoming carry chain signal of node $k-1$ is forwarded to the $MUXCY$ block of $k+1$. The 1-input of the first $MUXCY$ block is constantly set to '1'. An additional carry chain is used to build the conjunction of all column-ANDs. While, in principle, forming a global AND over all nodes is detrimental to scalability, my results show that a barrier synchronization of 256 nodes, arranged in a regular 16×16 mesh layout, can be achieved in less than 10ns ($\sim$100MHz) on a Xilinx Virtex-4 LX200-11 device.

In contrast to the barrier network, an interrupt network enables single nodes to initiate a control signal broadcast. The Picoblaze many-core architecture uses the interrupt network to manage a wakeup mechanism. A wakeup interrupt can be induced by any active note and is used to release nodes which are in sleep mode. Technically, the interrupt uses a very similar structure as the barrier network, but replaces the wide AND-gate by an OR-gate.

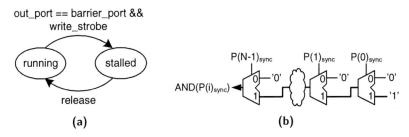

Figure 3.2: Barrier state machine of a PE (a) and carry chain implementation of the barrier net (b).

3.4 Resource Evaluation of Reconfigurable Mesh Many-Cores

The proposed many-cores have a tiled architecture, that is, they consist of a two-dimensional array of basically identical tiles. Figure 3.3(a) shows a general sketch of a 4×4 reconfigurable mesh. Each tile contains a PE and one or more network elements which connect the PEs to global communication infrastructures. If a reconfigurable mesh based interconnect is used, the network element is called a switch, packet-switched network elements are called routers. I have analyzed several many-core prototypes based on the building blocks presented in Sections 3.1 and 3.2 ranging from large scale reconfigurable mesh architectures of simple Picoblaze PEs to smaller scale architectures with powerful Microblaze PEs.

Figure 3.3(b) shows how a 4×4 many-core of Picoblaze based tiles is arranged. The reconfigurable mesh of Picoblaze cores operates as a coprocessor attached to a host processor system via a dedicated fast data link. On the coprocessor side, a communication controller feeds a number of data channels that can connect to the SEs at the border of the node array. In Figure 3.3(b), only the processor furthest to the left of each row is connected to the I/O interface. However, it is configurable at compile time which boundary nodes are attached to this communication interface. The Microblaze host can undertake sequential parts of an application and serves as a memory interface for the Picoblaze mesh. Data is transferred through an FSL channel to and from the mesh. For a write operation, the Microblaze transfers several 32-bit words to the FSL. The first 32-bit data word of the host is used to configure the I/O interface and includes information about the number of input and output bytes of the mesh. Following 32-bit words are then interpreted as sequence of 8-bit words for the Picoblaze array. In the example design of 3.3(b), a single Microblaze word would be converted into four 8-bit input

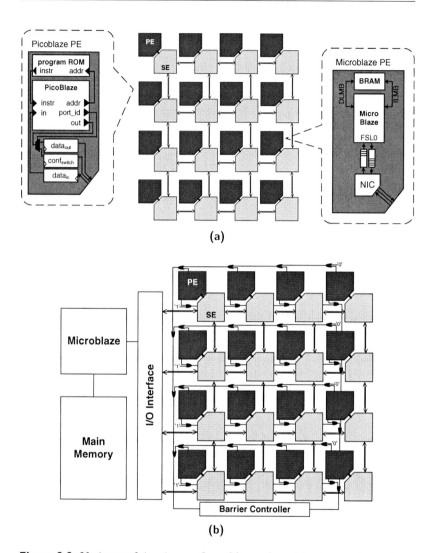

Figure 3.3: Variants of 4×4 reconfigurable mesh architectures: General reconfigurable mesh architecture sketch with the two possible PEs (a). A Picoblaze based design with left edge switches connected to a Microblaze host CPU through an I/O interface module and networks for barrier synchronization and interrupt control 3.3(b).

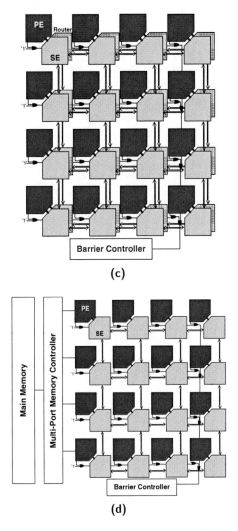

Figure 3.3: An architecture using Microblaze cores with PEs in the first column connected to external memory via Xilinx multi-port memory controller (c). A Microblaze based architecture with a hybrid data network (d). Both Microblaze meshes are equipped with a barrier synchronization network.

words for the mesh. When the sequencing of data for the current algorithm step is finished, the data is made visible to the mesh and injected by setting the valid bit to '1'. To keep the I/O interface and the mesh algorithm in synchrony, the barrier mechanism can be used. The barrier net is implemented as a wide AND-gate spanning all nodes and being evaluated by the barrier core. In almost the same manner, but using an OR function, the interrupt mechanism is realized.

In a many-core architecture using Microblaze PEs, every tile consists of at least a Microblaze PE and a SE. The Microblaze cores store their programs and data in local memory, which is implemented as BRAM memory inside the FPGA fabric. Shared data is communicated through the reconfigurable mesh based interconnect. Figures 3.3(c) and 3.3(d) show such Microblaze based many-core architectures, but both examples also reveal enhancements which go beyond the general setup. The architecture in 3.3(c) connects certain PEs to external memory through the multi-port memory controller shipped with the EDK suite. In general, possibilities to connect PEs to external memory are manifold. One typical setup is to connect a single PE to external memory and peripherals via a system bus. In Figure 3.3(c), the processors of the first column are connected directly to memory, whereas it is configurable if data should be cached or not. This way, the cores connected to main memory form a shared memory sub-system. Figure 3.3(d) extends the baseline many-core by an additional data network, which, in contrast to the reconfigurable mesh based network, uses packet-switching and wormhole routing for data transportation. As the Picoblaze variant, Microblaze based many-cores use a barrier net for synchronization. The network itself is the same for both alternatives, the network interface, however, is implemented in different ways. Where the Microblaze uses an FSL based interface to the barrier net, the barrier interface of the Picoblaze is encapsulated in the wrapper module (see Section 3.2).

3.4.1 Implementation Results for Picoblaze based Many-Cores

Table 3.3 shows implementation results for several basic modules and whole many-core prototypes that utilize the Picoblaze core as PE. To integrate a stall functionality into the Picoblaze core, only a single additional LUT is needed because most of the changes could be incorporated into the existent resources. While the register count of 36 flip-flops used for buffering 9-bit words at each of the four network outputs of the SEs stays constant for all versions, the 4-input LUT resources increase dramatically when using SEs that support more complex patterns. This is for two reasons: First, each additional pattern increases the complexity of multiplexers and, second, some patterns of more powerful models like RMESH need to combine multiple incoming ports which is done by forming a wired OR of the signals.

A single tile of the Picoblaze based reconfigurable mesh consumes roughly 130 flip-flops and from 270 to 492 LUTs, depending on the used switch model. In addition to the PE and the SE, a tile includes a BRAM block which is used as program memory. The critical path of a tile is on the connection of the BRAM and the Picoblaze core and limits the clock frequency to a maximum of 180 MHz. When composing a larger scale system out of mesh connected tiles, the achievable clock frequency does not decrease. This property clarifies the scalability of the interconnect as the whole system can run at the speed of a single node.

The device utilization linearly scales with the number of cores. Table 3.3 shows mesh sizes from 16 to 256 nodes. As every core needs a separate program memory, the amount of 336 BRAM blocks on the device becomes the limiting factor. The bottom row shows resource utilization for a complete prototype system including a 16×16 array of Picoblaze based PEs with RMESH switches and a Microblaze host system connected through a communication controller. The whole system was constrained to run with a global common clock at 100 MHz. Such a system stresses the LUT resources of the Virtex-4 LX200 device up to 71% and consumes 86% of the BRAMs.

Building block	Flip-Flops	4-input LUTs	BRAM	f_{max}
Picoblaze (kcpsm3)	76 (0.04%)	181 (0.10%)	1 (0.30%)	265
Picoblaze (w/ stall)	76 (0.04%)	182 (0.10%)	1 (0.30%)	265
Picoblaze PE	102 (0.06%)	209 (0.12%)	1 (0.30%)	242
HV-RN switch	36 (0.02%)	76 (0.04%)	0 (0.00%)	455
LRN switch	36 (0.02%)	157 (0.08%)	0 (0.00%)	351
RMESH switch	36 (0.02%)	290 (0.16%)	0 (0.00%)	308
HV-RN tile	131 (0.07%)	270 (0.15%)	1 (0.30%)	180
LRN tile	131 (0.07%)	344 (0.19%)	1 (0.30%)	180
RMESH tile	132 (0.07%)	492 (0.28%)	1 (0.30%)	180
4 × 4 RMESH	2'103 (1%)	6'837 (3%)	16 (4%)	180
8 × 8 RMESH	8'379 (5%)	28'812 (16%)	64 (19%)	180
16 × 16 RMESH	33'397 (19%)	121'145 (68%)	256 (76%)	180
16 × 16 Prototype: μBlaze + 16 × 16 RMESH	36'080 (20.24%)	126'555 (71.02%)	288 (85.71%)	100

Table 3.3: Resource utilization and clock rate (in MHz) for Picoblaze based many-core IP components synthesized for a Virtex-4 LX200/Speedgrade -11 FPGA device

Module	LUT	FF	DSP	BRAM
6×6 system	65495 (94%)	38776 (56%)	57 (89%)	139 (93%)
Microblaze (master node)	1298	1266	3	2
Microblaze (memory node)	1241	1162	3	2
Microblaze (worker node)	967	1021	3/0	0
Switch (RMESH)	446	132	0	0
Switch (HV-RN)	204	132	0	0
FSL interface to switch	5	38	0	0
Single 32x32Bit FIFO	65	17	0	0
FSL interface to barrier	6	3	0	0

Table 3.4: Virtex-5 LX110T resource utilization for design components.

3.4.2 Implementation Results for Microblaze based Many-Cores

Resource utilization results for Microblaze based many-core architectures are given using two system setups. The first prototype consists of a 6×6 array of Microblaze tiles running at 100MHz and was implemented on a Virtex-5 LX110T, speedgrade-1 device. The slice occupation for this design is 99%. Table 3.4 presents the resource utilization breakdown into LUTs, FFs, DSP blocks, and BRAMs. A single Microblaze PE occupies 967 to 1298 LUTs, depending on the node type. Nodes with access to external RAM are called *memory nodes*, and all other nodes *worker nodes*. A single *memory node* is denoted as *master node* and connects to a timer and further peripherals such as RS232 and a debug module via a processor local bus (PLB). As memory nodes have 2 kByte write-through data caches, they use more resources on the device. The master node is equipped with 32 kByte, other nodes with 4 kByte scratchpad memory for instructions and data. All the nodes' programs are stored in local memory and as the worker nodes do not have direct access to external memory, workers keep all their data sections in local scratchpad. A schematic of the system is depicted in Figure 3.3(b).

The resource utilization for 32-bit SEs highly depends on the supported patterns. An SE that can handle all RMESH patterns consumes 446 LUTs, a switch that can only apply horizontal and vertical buses (HV-RN) consumes 204 LUTs. In both cases, 132 flip-flops are used to buffer single words at the outgoing N, E, W and S ports. The interfaces to the fast simplex links consume rather few resources. An FSL interface for the data network occupies 5 LUTs and 38 flip flops. The additional two FIFOs are implemented in distributed RAM and consume 65 LUTs each. For the complete barrier mechanism, 6 LUTs and 3 flip flops are needed per node.

3.5 Chapter Conclusion

This chapter describes the architecture of reconfigurable mesh many-cores and their implementation in FPGA technology. The main part of the chapter deals with the building blocks of reconfigurable meshes. The multiplexer based SE can be configured to support various reconfigurable mesh models and data widths. Using a plain and well defined interface facilitates to couple various PEs and SEs. Here, I present two PE implementations: The first one utilizes a small footprint Picoblaze soft core as processing module which allows for implementing large scale meshes on single FPGA devices. The Picoblaze's deterministic instruction timing makes it possible to operate the array in a lock-step fashion. An alternative, more powerful PE uses the 32-bit Microblaze RISC core. Both PEs support global synchronization through a high-speed barrier network. For a 265 node reconfigurable mesh prototype, barrier synchronization causes a runtime overhead of 3 cycles using the FPGAs fast carry-chain capabilities.

CHAPTER 4

Programming of Reconfigurable Mesh Many-Cores

Programming parallel systems, no matter whether being assembled out of multiple computers or single chip multi-cores, is a challenging problem. In general, parallelism can be extracted from sequential codes automatically or, alternatively, the programmer has to express parallelism explicitly. For the reconfigurable mesh programming model, the explicit approach is preferred, as it is completely unexplored how to automatically derive reconfigurable mesh algorithms from existing sequential codes. This chapter deals with the question of implementing reconfigurable mesh algorithms on concrete many-core platforms. Issues of practical architectures and programming tool flows have not been sufficiently considered because the reconfigurable mesh has mainly been used as a theoretical vehicle. Also, as algorithms have typically been formulated in mathematical notations, there is almost no programming language which adequately covers the requirements of reconfigurable mesh algorithms. To address this issue, I developed the programming language ARMLang for the implementation of reconfigurable mesh programs, together with a compilation and debugging tool flow. ARMLang supports fine-grained program path equalization and is dedicated for rather simple PEs with deterministic instruction timing. For more powerful PEs, like the Microblaze core, the ARMLang features can be expressed by C statements and preprocessor directives. The last section of this chapter discusses the matter of debugging reconfigurable mesh programs.

4.1 Tool Flow Overview

The overall programming tool flow can be distincted in a hardware or platform generation part and in a software programming part. Both, the hardware and the software part rely on the Xilinx Embedded Development (EDK) tool flow. Figure 4.1 shows two variants of programming tool flows for the proposed many-core architectures.

The platform generation tool flow is completely integrated into the EDK suite. A Picoblaze based reconfigurable mesh is defined as a single parameterizable module, named *pcore* in the EDK terminology. An FSL connector attaches the mesh to a Microblaze host CPU. Settings for the Picoblaze reconfigurable mesh and the FSL interface can be specified within the EDK tool. Beside parameters like height and width of the array, also the type of the SEs can be declared. The programmer can chose among the HV-RN, the LRN, or the general RMESH switch. The complete hardwire environment is captured in a single specification file and processed by the Xilinx *platgen* tool. This process unveils the specification to a top-level VHDL design with parametrized instantiations of all sub-modules. After generating the platform description with platgen, synthesis tools are invoked to generate a netlist specification of the design. Finally, Xilinx mapping and place & route tools create a vendor-specific "Native Circuit Description" (NCD) file which defines the complete FPGA implementation of the many-core platform. For the Microblaze based many-core platform generation flow, I decided to not generate the mesh as a whole, but rather build single pcores for PEs and SEs. This approach allows for more flexibility and is very practical as all mesh entities use FIFO interfaces for communication. Since it is not convenient to manually connect a multitude of mesh elements in a proper way, a generator was developed used to automatically create platform specifications.

On the software side the programming tool flows for Picoblaze and Microblaze many-cores are more diverse. If the platform is configured to apply Microblaze PEs, all cores are programmed in C as shown in Figure 4.1(b). A benefit of this approach is that all compilation steps could be easily automated with the help of the EDK tool suite. If Picoblaze PEs are used, the parallel application is coded in ARMLang and the program of the Microblaze host is written in C like depicted in Figure 4.1(a). A detailed description of the programming flow for Picoblaze PEs is given in the following section. The corresponding flow for Microblaze PEs is described in Section 4.3.

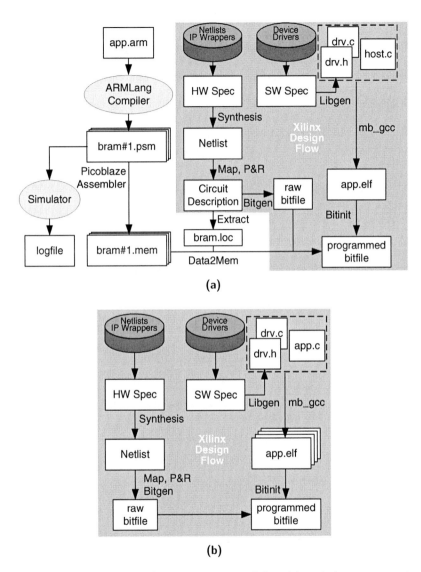

Figure 4.1: Picoblaze mesh programming tool flow (a) and the counterpart flow for many-cores with Microblaze PEs (b).

4.2 A Domain-specific Language for Time-deterministic PEs

The programming tool flow for Picoblaze based many-cores is sketched in Figure 4.1(a). For generating the executable for the Microblaze host processor the standard software development flow of the EDK environment is used. Generating code for the Picoblaze cores in the array is, however, more involved for two reasons. First, program code for each individual node in an array has to be generated and, ideally, the programmer should start with one single program specification. Second, there is no compiler available for the Picoblaze core. One could of course write an assembly language program for each of the cores. However, this is an extremely tedious task and becomes totally impracticable when one tries to manually equalize paths lengths in the different programs. To overcome these hurdles, I have developed a new language ARMLang to specify reconfigurable mesh algorithms and a corresponding compiler.

As shown in Figure 4.1(a), the ARMLang compiler creates a separate assembly file for each Picoblaze node out of a single specification file. In a second step, the Picoblaze assembler tool is invoked on each assembly program in order to spill machine code in form of memory files. Finally, the *Data2Mem* tool of the EDK suite is used to merge the memory files into the FPGA bitstream. To automatize the whole process of compilation and bitstream modification, a shell script was developed that instruments several Xilinx command line tools. For example, the position of the Picoblazes' program ROMs has to be extracted out of the NCD description of the FPGA design. Alternatively, one could constrain the placement of these block RAMs before synthesis, and use the beforehand known positions during bitfile modification. However, my experiments have shown that better synthesis results can be achieved by leaving block RAM placement to the Xilinx tool flow.

As a variant of the regular programming flow an additional simulation flow was developed (c.f. Section 4.4). The simulator consists of a Picoblaze instruction set simulator and a reconfigurable mesh simulator that handles data transportation among cores. An advantage of the simulation flow is that the simulated meshes can be of much larger size than those implementable on a single FPGA devices. The simulator reads the assembly files created by the ARMLang compiler and generates a log-file during a simulation run. A visualizer tool with a graphical interface helps the programmer to debug the algorithm by trace analysis.

4.2.1 ARMLang

This section describes the language ARMLang, together with syntax and semantics of some of its statements. I decided to develop a new language because earlier presented reconfigurable mesh languages such as PPC [103] or RMPC [122] are either dedicated to simulation or are only suited for a specific mesh model. On the other hand, current and emerging parallel languages like HPF [84] or Unified Parallel C [40] are intended as more general programming languages. They typically hide inter processor communication from the programmer and make distributed memory look like global shared memory. This approach does not fit the reconfigurable mesh programming model which heavily utilizes fine-grained communication.

While the hardware architecture is essentially influenced by the reconfigurable mesh model, ARMLang is designed to support a broader class of programming models. The language is able to express algorithms that follow the principles of lockstep execution for regular processor arrays. Besides the reconfigurable mesh, also systolic arrays and cellular automata lead to algorithms with that characteristic and can thus be supported by ARMLang. Unlike the general SIMD model, the architectures described in this thesis do not impose the restriction to globally execute a single instruction. PEs autonomously execute dedicated programs on local data while the overall algorithm proceeds synchronously in terms of steps.

In contrast to the vast majority of parallel programming models, communication partners can not be directly addressed in ARMLang. Rather, communication can only be done via broadcasting to local bus segments. However, by properly reconfiguring their local switches, the PEs are able to build various global communication patterns. For example, pairs of cores can isolate themselves from the rest of the array, effectively allowing for a huge number of parallel communications.

Listing 4.1 shows an essential part of the BackusNaur Form (BNF) representation of ARMLang. The Program rule expresses the top-level structure of an ARMLang specification which comprises three parts. First, the programmer specifies the name and the dimensions of the program. For example, the ARMLang statement PROGRAM Sort(8:8); defines a program named *Sort* for an 8×8 array of nodes. Consequently, the ARMLang compiler will generate 64 individual programs. The second part of an ARMLang program is the variables declaration. Variables can be either scalar values or arrays. Following the reconfigurable mesh programming model, all data in ARMLang is completely distributed providing each processor with its own local copy of all variables. The final part of an ARMLang program is the program body,

```
Program   ::= "PROGRAM" Ident "(" Number ":" Number ")" ";"
              "DECLARE" DeclLst "BEGIN" StatSeq "END" "." .
DeclLst   ::= Decl | Decl ";" DeclLst .
Decl      ::= Ident ":" Type .
Type      ::= Scalar | Vector .
Scalar    ::= "INTEGER" .
Vector    ::= "ARRAY" "[" Number ".." Number "]" "OF" Scalar.
StatSeq   ::= Stat | StatSeq ";" Stat .
Stat      ::= "SYNC"
|  "WHERE" PIDRelation "DO" StatSeq "END"
|  "WHERE" PIDRelation "DO" StatSeq "ELSEWHERE" StatSeq "END"
|  "IF" Relation "THEN" StatSeq "ELSE" StatSeq "END"
|  "IF" Relation "THEN" StatSeq "END"
|  "WHILE" Relation "DO" StatSeq "END"
|  "FOR" "(" Stat ";" Relation ";" Stat ")" "DO" StatSeq "END"
|  "SWITCH" SWConf
|  "WAIT" "(" PIDExpression ")"
|  Assignment
|  "READ" "(" Desig "," Expr0 ")" | "READ" "(" Desig ")"
|  "WRITE" "(" Desig "," Expr0 ")" | "WRITE" "(" Desig ")" .
SWConf    := "VOID" | "NS" | "WE" | "NW" | "NE"
|  "SE" | "SW" | "NWS" | "NWE" | "NES" | "ESW"
|  "NSWE" | "N" | "S" | "W" | "E" .
```

Listing 4.1: BNF fragment of the ARMLang language.

formed by a sequence of statements.

ARMLang supports a variety of statements known from standard programming languages, but also some very distinctive statements specific to the reconfigurable mesh model. Among the familiar statements are assignments using the variables, a number of arithmetic operators and the assignment operator ":=". Control flow is coded with the familiar IF and IF-ELSE constructs or, for loops, with WHILE and FOR statements. Line comments are started with double slashes. ARMLang's more distinctive statements are described in the following.

Node Distinction: Besides the normal control flow statements, ARMLang supports a second class of conditional statements used for program generation. The WHERE and WHERE-ELSEWHERE constructs capture statements that should be executed only on certain groups of PEs. Thus, the conditions of the WHERE and WHERE-ELSEWHERE statements have to be evaluated at compile time. These conditions are denoted as *PIDRelations*, and can be formed out of numbers and static parameters such as processors identifiers (PID), the overall number of processors (CORES), or the array's dimensions (WIDTH and HEIGHT).

Communication: The interconnect of the reconfigurable mesh many-core bases on reconfigurable switches attached to the PEs. To support communication, ARMLang includes a SWITCH statement which the PE executes to set the switch pattern for its local SE, as well as READ and WRITE statements for the actual communication. The SWITCH statement requires as parameter one of the allowed switch settings (*SWConf*), which are shown in Listing 4.1. For example, the pattern NWS indicates that the north, the west and the south port of the SE need to be fused. Additionally, the PE is connected to the resulting bus segment. Hence, a subsequent READ operation reads in data that has passed the switch through the fused ports. The example given in Listing 4.2, code fragment #1, shows a simple sequence of a WRITE and a READ statement which allows two nodes to exchange values. This code assumes that pairs of processing elements have been connected by proper switch settings. Otherwise, these statements would lead to multiple writes on a single bus segment. Both connected PEs can execute WRITE and READ simultaneously, as the architecture employs communication channels with directed links.

Path Equalization & Timing: As discussed in Section 3.2.2, the architecture and machine model supports fine-grained program path equalization as a first synchronization mode. This synchronization mode is applicable to PEs with deterministic timing, i.e., without caching and pipelining effects. Examples are algorithmic state machines or the Picoblaze processor that is used as PE in one of the proposed many-core architectures in this thesis.

Figure 4.2 provides examples for how ARMLang supports synchronization. Without path balancing the compiler would generate separate programs that are not synchronized, as depicted in 4.2(a). If path balancing is applied, the ARMLang compiler traverses all possible program paths and pads the shorter sub-paths of conditional branches. In case of, e.g., a basic if-statement, the compiler automatically adds an else-branch which is filled with no-operation (NOP) instructions. Thus, the runtime of the whole if-statement consumes always the same amount of time, regardless of the result the dynamic if-condition evaluates to. To compact code size, the ARMLang compiler replaces longer sequences of NOP instructions by loops over NOP instructions.

Figure 4.2(b) shows how the program paths of multiple cores get balanced through the insertion of NOP instructions. To adjust timing by hand, the programmer has the option to use a WAIT statement. This statement requires an expression as parameter that evaluates to a certain number of NOP instructions to be inserted. The main use case for WAIT instructions is to manually influence the communication timing. In Figure 4.2(b), the insertion of NOP instructions caused by WAIT statements is depicted by dashed lines. In every communication phase, each reader node has to wait a certain amount of cycles before it is assured that broadcasted data has arrived. Thus, the reader nodes schedule a wait statement ahead of a read instruction. The remaining NOPs are inserted due to the path equalization method. The figure shows, that all computation phases are padded to be of equal length. Additionally, NOP instructions are scheduled in the sequel of broadcasts operations. This is because the communication phase is typically implemented by means of a WHERE-ELSEWHERE statement. If the WHERE part comprises only a broadcast operation and the ELSEWHERE part a WAIT statement followed up by a READ instruction, the WHERE part is padded with NOPs to run exactly as long as the ELSEWHERE counterpart.

Code fragment #2 in Listing 4.2 gives an example for broadcasting values. The top-left node of the array, the one with processor identifier 0, writes the variable a to its local bus segment. All the other nodes of the array execute a NOP instruction which has been inserted into their code by the compiler. Then, every core executes WIDTH*HEIGHT no-operation instructions before all cores with an identifier greater than 0 read the received value. This code fragment assumes that the switches have been set properly to establish a global linear bus structure.

Barrier Synchronization: As a second means of synchronization which is also applicable to more complex PEs with non-deterministic instruction timing, ARMLang supports barrier synchronization. Barrier synchronization can be achieved by the SYNC statement. Executing such a statement immediately stalls the PE and drives a logical 1 onto the barrier network. A controller waits until all PEs have raised their signal on the barrier network and then broadcasts a continue signal back to the cores. Figure 4.2(c) shows an example trace for barrier synchronization. In contrast to path equalization, communication phases and computation phases can be interleaved. Writer nodes do not have to wait for the reader nodes to finish their READ operation and can continue productive computation immediately after broadcasting. However, barrier synchronization also comes with an overhead which is due to the insertion of SYNC instructions.

Code fragment #3 in Listing 4.2 presents an example for the use of the SYNC statement. Using the SYNC statement, the programmer ensures that all cores have completed their WRITE statements before any core executes its READ statement.

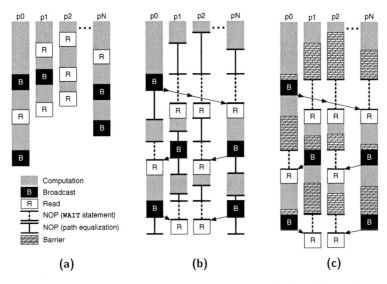

Figure 4.2: Comparison of two synchronization methods. The parallel program (a) can be synchronized by path equalization (b) and barrier synchronization (c).

```
// code fragment #1
WRITE(a);
READ(a);

// code fragment #2
WHERE PID==0 DO
  WRITE(a)
END;
WAIT(WIDTH*HEIGHT);
WHERE PID>0 DO
  READ(a)
END;

// code fragment #3
IF (a>b) THEN WRITE(a) END;
SYNC;
IF (a<b) THEN READ(a) END;
```

Listing 4.2: Three communication patterns.

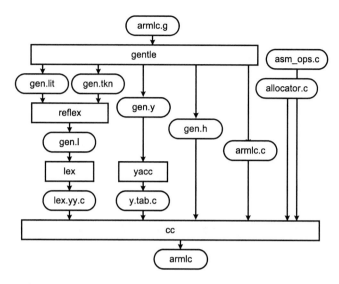

Figure 4.3: GENTLE tool flow for the `armlc` example.

4.2.2 ARMLang Compiler

I have decided to utilize the compiler specification framework GENTLE [144] in order to create a compiler that translates ARMLang programs into Xilinx Picoblaze assembly language. As ARMLang is still in the state of flux and it should be possible to target other processor cores as well, one can greatly benefit from such a compiler compiler because it allows for rather fast design iterations, for example, from changes in the language specification to the generation of a new compiler.

GENTLE is a compiler construction system developed at GMD research labs which comprises a specification language and tools for generating all phases of a compiler out of high-level descriptions. GENTLE originates in Kees Koster's Compiler Description Language (CDL) [87] and PROLOG. The logic programming approach underlying GENTLE rests upon the principle of locality which allows to compose all compiler phases out of a set of local rules.

Figure 4.3 shows the overall GENTLE tool flow that translates from a specification in form of a GENTLE module (`armlc.g`) to the target compiler executable (`armlc`). A GENTLE specification involves type definitions, production rules and transformation rules. Starting with such a specification,

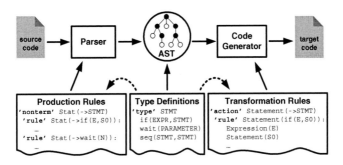

Figure 4.4: Compiler specification.

the gentle tool produces a number of intermediate specification files. These files include scanner specifications for terminal symbols (gen.lit) and tokens (gen.tkn), a Yacc specification of the underlying grammar (gen.y), a C header file that introduces a data type for token attributes and defines the codes for the tokens (gen.h), and a C file containing code for the remaining functions of the target compiler, in particular the code generator. The reflex tool produces the final specification for the generation of a scanner (gen.l). The GENTLE flow then invokes the well-known UNIX programs Lex and Yacc to generate source code for scanner and parser for the target language. GENTLE also allows to specify rules only by their prototype, and to include an implementation of the corresponding functions in C. In the ARMLang compiler, register allocation is completely implemented in C (asm_ops.c and allocator.c) rather than in GENTLE itself. Finally, a C compiler generates the target compiler executable.

The specification of a compiler in GENTLE basically consists of a parser specification, an abstract syntax definition, and a set of transformation rules for code generation. Figure 4.4 shows the compiler phases and the required specifications for each phase. The GENTLE specification of a parser is given as a set of production rules which define the grammar for the language to be processed. By successfully expanding these rules on the incoming source code, an abstract syntax tree (AST) is constructed. The actual AST construction bases on type definitions. Types are also useful to check the consistency of the production rules. Finally, transformation rules allow for restructuring the AST and generating target code.

In the following, the specifications that drive the generation of the three phases of a compiler are exemplified by (incomplete) small fragments of the GENTLE specification for the ARMLang language:

Parser Specification: The parser analyzes incoming code syntactically and transforms it into an abstract representation. The context free grammar of the language to be processed consists of nonterminal symbols and tokens. While tokens stand for themselves, nonterminal symbols have to be expanded by certain rules. Listing 4.3 shows production rules for the nonterminal symbols `StatSeq` and `Stat`. All rules that belong to a certain symbol represent alternative ways to expand that symbol. In this example, two alternative rules for the `StatSeq` symbol are given. Using the first rule, the parser will try to expand a `StatSeq` symbol according to rules of the `Stat` symbol. In the event of successful expansion, the `Stat` rule returns an abstract node `S` which is also returned by the `StatSeq` rule. If such a matching is not successful, the parser will retry to expand the current node, but now in form of a concatenation of a `StatSeq` symbol, the token ";" and a symbol of type `Stat`. Finally, a sequence of statements will be expanded to a binary tree, where each right node is of kind `Stat`.

```
'nonterm' StatSeq(-> STMT)
'rule' StatSeq(-> S) : Stat(-> S)
'rule' StatSeq(-> seq(S1, S2)) :
  StatSeq(-> S1) ";" Stat(-> S2)

'nonterm' Stat(-> STMT)
'rule' Stat(-> wait(P)) : "WAIT" "(" PIDParam(-> P) ")"
'rule' Stat(-> ifelse(E, S1, S2)) : "IF" Relation(-> E)
  "THEN" StatSeq(-> S1)  "ELSE" StatSeq(-> S2) "END"
```

Listing 4.3: Parser specification.

GENTLE analyzes the specification and invokes Yacc to convert the context-free grammar of the language definition into an LALR(1) parser for that grammar. The result of parsing is an abstract syntax tree which can be further processed by means of semantic analysis and, finally, code generation.

Type Definitions: In GENTLE, the abstract syntax of a language is given in form of so-called type definitions. Each type consists of a name and a list of alternatives for its shape. Listing 4.4 shows a specification fragment for a type named `STMT`. Each node of the AST that is of this type can take the shape of several alternatives, among them are `wait(PARAMETER)`, `ifelse(EXPR, STMT, STMT)` or `seq(STMT, STMT)`. While the parser expands the production rules, it emits nodes and creates the program's AST. Depending on which of the alternative rules for a symbol can be applied, the result of the expansion varies. For the example in Listing 4.3, the production rule for `Stat` returns a `STMT` node, either of type `wait` or of type `ifelse`. These shapes determine, how the subtree of the AST node is structured, e.g., if a STMT node is of type `ifelse`, it has three direct successors, one EXPR and two a STMT nodes.

```
'type' STMT
  wait(PARAMETER)
  ifelse(EXPR, STMT, STMT)
  seq(STMT, STMT)
  [...]
```

Listing 4.4: Type definition.

Code Generator: The final phase of the ARMLang compiler is the target code generation. GENTLE allows for specifying rules for processing the AST, prior generated by the parser. For transformation purposes, rules of a different kind, called *action rules*, are used. Whereas `nonterm` production rules are selected according to the structure of the concrete input, rules for `action` predicates are selected according to the structure of the abstract syntax. While the rule-selection strategy used for `nonterm` predicates is based on a LALR(1) parsing algorithm, predicates of the category `action` are evaluated by shallow backtracking.

While the previous phases of creating the parser and the AST are fairly standard, the code generator for ARMLang is special in that it creates code for all processors of the array. Basically, code is generated by traversing or un-parsing the AST. Similar to the parser specification by `nonterm` rules, the code generator is specified by `action` rules. Listing 4.5 presents rules for the `Translate` statement. The input for both rules is an abstract syntax term `dcl(N, Ident, Prog)`, where N is an integer, `Ident` an identifier storing the program's name and `Prog` a more complex subtree containing the abstract syntax of the parsed program.

```
'rule' Translate(dcl(N, Ident, Prog)) :
  GetCORES(-> M) gt(N,M)

'rule' Translate(dcl(N, Ident, Prog)):
  Generate(dcl(N, Ident, Prog))
  RegAllocate(N)
  Translate(dcl(N+1, Ident, Prog))
```

Listing 4.5: Translation rules.

The first rule for `Translate` starts with expanding the `GetCORES` predicate which returns `M`, the overall number of cores in the array. Then, the predicate `gt(N,M)` is expanded which indicates whether the first parameter is greater than the second. If not, the predicate can not be successfully expanded and the backtracking mechanism will select the next rule for expansion. The second rule for `Translate` first expands the `Generate` predicate which transforms the abstract syntax into an intermediate representation for processor `N`. While the syntax of the intermediate representation is similar to the instruction set of the Picoblaze processor, it differs by its use of temporal instead of concrete registers names. Then, a second predicate `RegAllocate` is expanded which realizes register allocation. In distinction from e.g., the `Generate` predicate, `RegAllocate` refers to a function written in C. Finally, the `Translate` predicate invokes a recursive call with `N+1` instead of `N` as first parameter. Hence, starting `Translate` with `N = 1`, the rule will generate code for every processor of the array. The first rule for `Translate` effectively terminates the recursion.

In GENTLE, the overall organization of the compiler is expressed by a single root clause. For example, the ARMLang specification includes the root clause:

```
'root' Program(->P) Translate(P).
```

The statement `Program(->P)` calls the actual parser on the input and returns a result `P`, which is handed over to the `Translate` statement. The placeholder `P` represents the root node of the AST.

GENTLE's backtracking mechanism, inherited from PROLOG, can also be used to elegantly implement instruction scheduling for balancing program path lengths within the ARMLang code generator. Listing 4.6 sketches the action rules for the abstract syntax term `where(E, S1)`. Here, `E` refers to the condition of the `WHERE` statement which can be evaluated at compile time. To this end, the predicate `PidCheck` transforms the static expression `E` into an integer value `I`, indicating the Boolean result of the conditional. If the result evaluates to true, the body of the `where` statement in the source code must be executed. Consequently, the predicate `Statement(S1)` is expanded. Otherwise, the second `Statement` rule starts to expand the predicate `ShadowStatement`. For every predicate that can be expanded by a `Statement` rule, a shadow version exists. The shadow predicates count the number of instructions that would be spilled by their original counterparts. Hereby, the output parameter `N` gives the number of instructions used to execute `S1`. The predicate `FNOP(N)` then schedules a sequence of `N` no-operation instructions into the intermediate representation of the program.

```
'action' Statement(STMT)
'rule' Statement(where(E, S1)) :
  PidCheck(E -> I)
  eq(I, 1)
  Statement(S1)

'rule' Statement(where(E, S1)) :
  ShadowStatement(S1 -> N)
  FNOP(N)
```

Listing 4.6: Rules for expanding a `where` statement.

4.2.3 ARMLang Code Examples

This section presents two simple example algorithms in ARMLang, first odd-even transposition sort and, second, maximum finding. The program odd-eventrans shown in Listing 4.7(a) uses 8×8 nodes for sorting 64 numbers. For the sake of brevity, it is assumed that each node already holds one of the values to be sorted in the variable a. As odd-even transposition sort works on linear arrays, I apply a snake-like indexing scheme to linearize the two-dimensional array of PEs. The rows of the array are numbered, beginning with 0 for the top row. The left-most node of row 0 is assigned an index of 0. Then, scanning through all rows, nodes in even rows are indexed in ascending order, while nodes in odd rows are indexed in descending order. The parameter SNAKEPID is used in the program to denote the position of a node in this snake-like ordered array.

Odd-even transposition sort iteratively compares the data of neighboring nodes and, if necessary, exchanges them. This is done for all node pairs in parallel [86]. The algorithm starts with connecting all even nodes with their adjoining neighbors with higher SNAKEPID. Every core with an even SNAKEPID connects itself to the east port, every other core connects itself to the west port of its local SE. This reconfiguration primitive is implemented by the macro SNAKE_ORDER_EVEN depicted in Listing 4.7(a). A similar macro SNAKE_ORDER_ODD is used to connect all odd nodes with their next neighbors. This macro is more involved because only a part of the node pairs are connected through their west and east ports. The remaining (boundary) nodes are connected through their north and south ports.

Sorting N numbers on an array of size N takes exactly N steps, alternating between the even and odd switch connection patterns. Thus, the program executes a FOR loop **CORES**/2 = N/2 times. In the loop body, first the even connection pattern is applied. Thus, each even node, according to the

SNAKEPID parameter that starts at index 0, configures itself to be connected
to the core with the next higher SNAKEPID. Then, pairs of nodes exchange
their values a by simultaneously writing a onto the bus and reading in the
received value t with the next instruction. According to their SNAKEPID, the
nodes save the minimum or maximum value into a. In the following step, the
odd connection pattern is applied and, again, the pairs exchange their values
if necessary. It has to be noted that the program shown in Listing 4.7(a)
makes no assumption about the size of the array, except that the number of
columns and rows must be even. By simply changing the WIDTH and HEIGHT
parameters in the PROGRAM declaration, the array size can be scaled.

```
#define SNAKE_ORDER_EVEN  \
  WHERE PID%2==0 DO \
    SWITCH E \
  ELSEWHERE \
    SWITCH W \
  END


PROGRAM oddeventrans(8:8);
DECLARE
  a : INTEGER; i : INTEGER;
  t : INTEGER
BEGIN
  FOR (i:=0;i<CORES/2;i:=i+1) DO
    SNAKE_ORDER_EVEN;
    WRITE(a);
    READ(t);
    WHERE (SNAKEPID%2)==0 DO
      IF a<t THEN a:=t END
    ELSEWHERE
      IF t<a THEN a:=t END
    END;
    SNAKE_ORDER_ODD;
    WHERE (SNAKEPID%(WIDTH*HEIGHT-1)
        )!=0 DO
      WRITE(a);
      READ(t);
      WHERE (SNAKEPID%2)==0 DO
        IF a<t THEN a:=t END
      ELSEWHERE
        IF t<a THEN a:=t END
      END
    END
  END
END.
```

(a)

```
PROGRAM Max(8:8);
DECLARE
  a : INTEGER; t : INTEGER
BEGIN
//Values to compare placed
//on the diagonal processors
  SWITCH WE;
  WHERE PID%(WIDTH+1)==0 DO
    WRITE(a)
  ELSEWHERE
    WAIT(WIDTH);
    READ(a)
  END;
  SWITCH NS;
  WHERE PID%(WIDTH+1)==0 DO
    WRITE(a)
  ELSEWHERE
    WAIT(HEIGHT);
    READ(t)
  END;
  WHERE PID%(WIDTH+1)!=0 DO
    IF (t<a) THEN
      WRITE(1)
    ELSE
      WRITE(0)
    END
    a := 0
  ELSEWHERE
    WAIT(HEIGHT);
    READ(t);
    IF (t==1) THEN a := 0 END
  END
END.
```

(b)

Listing 4.7: Linear array odd-even transposition sort (a) and reconfigurable
mesh maximum algorithm (b).

As a second example, an ARMLang program for finding the maximum [113] is presented in Listing 4.7(b). The algorithm finds the maximum of N values on an $N \times N$ reconfigurable mesh. Again, is is assumed for brevity that the N values have been preloaded into the local variables a of the diagonal nodes.

The first step configures row buses in the array by invoking the SWITCH WE instruction. Then, nodes on the diagonal, checked for by the expression PID%(WIDTH+1)==0, broadcast their values to the bus. All other nodes wait for WIDTH cycles before reading the bus. After the first WHERE–ELSEWHERE block all nodes in a row hold the same value a. By properly generating target code, the ARMLang compiler guarantees that all nodes are synchronous. In the following lines, the array is configured to install column buses. Then, again, the diagonal processors broadcast their values a and the other nodes read this values into their variables t.

In the third WHERE–ELSEWHERE block, all non-diagonal nodes compare the value t with the earlier read value a. Let us denote such a node as i. If t < a, the diagonal node lying on the same row as i holds a greater value than the diagonal node lying on the same column as i. Thus, node i writes a 1 onto the column bus to inform the diagonal processor to invalidate its a variable. This is done by all non-diagonal nodes concurrently. At the end, the maximum is hold by the diagonal node with value a greater than 0.

4.3 A C-level Programming Flow for Barrier-Synchronized Many-Cores

The EDK framework includes a GNU C/C++ tool chain for the Microblaze core. As the C language is generally more powerful than ARMLang, it is desirable to use the existing C toolflow instead of developing a Microblaze backend for ARMLang. However, ARMLang has several constructs (c.f. Section 4.2.1) which are not delivered in C by default. To address this issue, I have developed C constructs that implement the same functionality as ARMLang's distinctive features:

- For **node distinction** in the Microblaze toolflow, preprocessor #if-directives are used to replace the WHERE construct of ARMLang. With the aid of the cores ID number XPAR_CPU_ID the array can be divided in groups of nodes which might all execute a different sequence of instructions. This allows for specifying the parallel algorithm in a single source file. During compilation, the preprocessor extracts the proper parts of the program for the desired core.

- **Communication** comprises two parts, switch reconfiguration and bus access. Switch reconfiguration in C is done by two subsequent instructions. First, the actual switch pattern is stored to an integer variable, e.g., by the instruction s = NS. Second, the switch pattern is written to the reconfigurable mesh network interface (port 0) by a control-labeled FSL *put* instruction: `putfslx(s,0,FSL_CONTROL)`. Bus access is handled by normal *put* or *get* instructions to the network interface.

- **Path equalization** is not used, because the timing of Microblaze cores is non-deterministic. To synchronize supersteps and communication phases, barrier synchronization is used. Additionally, **timing** does not have to be manually influenced to wait for incoming data. If the program satisfies the communication rules as stated in Section 3.2.3, the blocking FSL *get* instructions automatically stall the cores until data is at hand.

- **Barrier synchronization** is the essential synchronization mechanism for the Microblaze based many-core. The `sync` macro is expanded to two subsequent FSL instructions. A *put* signals the arrival of the barrier to the global barrier net. The following blocking *get* stalls the core until the barrier controller broadcasts a continuation signal.

I have developed a minimal API for accessing the NoC, reconfigurable mesh and barrier networks. Table 4.1 shows C macros for transmitting and receiving integer and float values, respectively. Additionally, single- and multi-word communication routines are distinguished. *Send* and *Receive* primitives are used to communicate via the NoC. When communicating through the reconfigurable mesh based network, *broadcasts* and *read* operations are applied to write to local bus segments and read from local bus segments, respectively. Receive and read operations have blocking semantics, i.e., a processor that initiates a blocking read on an FSL link gets stalled, until valid data is present in the FSL's incoming FIFO. The proper setting of bus switches is handled by means of the *swconf* primitive, whereas *sync* schedules a barrier synchronization point into the core's program.

4.4 Debugging

The development of parallel programs is typically an error-prone task and consequently, a compilation tool flow should include a means for debugging. In particular for the very fine-grained Picoblaze based reconfigurable mesh, which affords synchronicity at a machine cycle level, dedicated debugging

Communication primitive	Summary
send(T,D)	Send single value[1] D through NoC to destination T
sendMsg(T,*D,L)	Send message D of L values through NoC
receive(*S)	Returns a single value received from the NoC. The optional parameter S indicates the sender node
receiveMsg(*D,*S)	Receives a message D from node S and returns the length of the message
swconf(P)	Reconfigure local SE to install pattern P
broadcast(D)	Broadcast value D to local bus segment
broadcastMsg(*D,L)	Broadcast message D of L values to local bus segment
read()	Read single value D from switch NIC buffer
read(*D,L)	Read sequence D of L values from switch NIC buffer
sync	Synchronize through barrier net

[1]Supported data types are integer and float

Table 4.1: Communication API primitives.

mechanisms are essential. To this end, a simulation framework was developed which allows for simulation and visualization of ARMLang programs. For the coarser-grained Microblaze PEs a self-developed separate debugging flow does not yet exist. However, the EDK framework includes comprehensive capabilities for debugging Microblaze based designs. On the hardware level, the programmer can generate thorough simulation models for a structural or behavioral hardware simulation. For software debugging, the Xilinx Microprocessor Debugger (XMD) tool can be used to connect to processors within the FPGA device. The programmer can choose among two alternative debugging facilities. A software handler (stub) that runs on the processor itself can be used to install a communication channel via serial IO to the XMD tool. The debug stub allows for performing basic debug operations like reading and writing memory and register values and controlling the program execution. A more powerful method for debugging is provided by the Microblaze Debug Module (MDM) which enables JTAG-based debugging of up to eight Microblaze processors in system. This way, the debugging occurs directly in hardware and does not need software intervention.

Debugging of ARMLang algorithms for the Picoblaze mesh is more sophisticated due to the fine-grained synchronization. In-circuit debugging is not favorable as it would be necessary to observe very large number of cores to get the required information about the global state of the mesh. On the other hand, full hardware simulation is too time consuming and on very low level of abstraction, e.g., waveform information has typically to be interpreted manually. For this reason, I have decided to use a high-level functional simulation of the Picoblaze based many-cores. The simulator is intended to help debugging reconfigurable mesh programs, but was also very valuable for the development of the ARMLang compiler. As the compiler was co-developed with the hardware architecture, the simulation framework was used to analyze the compiler's target code generator.

The Picoblaze reconfigurable mesh simulator comprises two parts, a Picoblaze instruction set simulator (PicoSim) and an underlying mesh simulator (RMeshSim). Both simulators have been written in Java. The PEs are encapsulated by generic wrapper modules, which facilitates the integration of other cycle-accurate processor simulators. A simulation run reads in the assembly code of the cores processors and generates a logfile output which documents the cores state at run-time. At each simulation step, the processor simulators execute one instruction for each PE in the array. Then, the network simulator realizes the transportation of data through the reconfigurable mesh. The network simulator can work in one of two modes. In the first mode, data travels exactly one hop per cycle modeling a pipelined network that uses buffered SEs. The second mode models single-cycle broadcasts on the bus segments which is applicable for combinational SEs. While in the first mode, time proceeds in discrete time steps, the second mode relies on a discrete-event simulation kernel.

The simulator allows for executing reconfigurable mesh algorithms and gather runtime measurements for arrays of arbitrary dimensions. The generated logfile comprises the complete states of all cores at any step of the executed algorithm. The logfiles are huge, easily in the order of several dozens of mega bytes. A graphical tool is indispensable for analyzing such an amount of data. Hence a graphical frontend for the simulator was developed that allows the programmer to visualize and browse all algorithms steps. A screenshot of the frontend is shown in Figure 4.5. In the main frame, the reconfigurable mesh is depicted and the states of the individual cores as well as the switch configurations are shown. These states can be tracked through the algorithm either in single step mode or by simulating up to certain time steps. This simulation and debugging environment greatly simplifies the detection of programming errors, the most subtle of which manifest themselves by broken synchronicity or inaccurately configured bus segments.

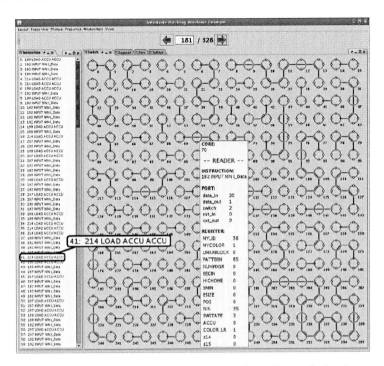

Figure 4.5: Graphical frontend for the reconfigurable mesh simulator.

4.5 Chapter Conclusion

In this chapter I have presented how reconfigurable mesh many-cores can be programmed and debugged. For the complex Microblaze cores that already support a high-level programming flow the programmer can specify reconfigurable mesh algorithms by using simple preprocessor directives for node distinction and a lightweight API for data communication and barrier synchronization. For the finer-grained Picoblaze processors that facilitate synchronization at instruction granularity I propose a dedicated programming flow based on the new language ARMLang. ARMLang is intended as a small language for programming on-chip multiprocessor arrays following certain programming models such as the reconfigurable mesh, cellular and systolic programming. Albeit the ARMLang compiler is not fully optimized, it allows for programming reconfigurable mesh programs on a reasonably high abstraction level. Using the GENTLE framework the complete ARMLang compiler is specified in a very compact manner. The entire ARMLang specification in GENTLE and C comprises 3400 lines of code. Out of this specification, GENTLE produces the compiler sources which incorporate more than 20'000 lines of code. The proposed many-cores can be debugged by means of conventional techniques like behavioral hardware simulation or in circuit debugging. Additionally, I have presented a customized simulation framework for Picoblaze based reconfigurable meshes. The simulator provides for studying large scale meshes in a cycle accurate manner and allows for debugging reconfigurable mesh algorithms in a descriptive way.

CHAPTER 5

Evaluation of Reconfigurable Mesh Many-Cores

In this chapter, the proposed FPGA many-core prototype implementations are evaluated in terms of performance, scalability and robustness. First, I present runtime experiments for typical compute-intensive kernels of different application domains. To this end, large scale meshes with Picoblaze PEs are compared to various single core systems. A second scenario studies the reconfigurable mesh network as interconnect for a 36-core Microblaze system. Using a matrix-matrix multiplication case study, the performance of the reconfigurable mesh many-core is compared to that of a 6-core shared memory system. Sections 5.2 and 5.3 deal with the aspects of robustness and scalability, respectively. I present a method to identify faulty nodes in the reconfigurable mesh and form a healthy sub-mesh out of the remaining operational nodes. Finally, I provide several results on self-simulation for reconfigurable mesh many-cores.

5.1 Runtime Results

5.1.1 Picoblaze Case Studies

In this section, I present four algorithmic kernels to illustrate the power of reconfigurable meshes. For each of the application domains arithmetic, sorting & selection, graph algorithms and imaging, a case study compares a reconfigurable mesh algorithm to a sequential solution. The reconfigurable mesh algorithms are implemented in ARMLang and executed on a Picoblaze-based many-core prototype and the cycle accurate simulator. I have implemented a sequential counterpart in C for each of the four applications and executed them on a single Microblaze core. Additionally, the C implementations are translated to an ARMLang specification by hand and compiled to a single Picoblaze executable with the ARMLang compiler. For the single core case studies, both, the Microblaze and the Picoblaze processor are solely connected to local (on-chip) memory to avoid memory access latencies. The major part of the sequential Picoblaze algorithms was run on the simulator because the core only supports up to 64 bytes of data storage in local scratchpad RAM, which is too little for most of the problem sizes. The simulator implements the Picoblaze ISA but can support wider data and memory than the hardware implementation. Runtime improvements of the parallel versions compared to the sequential Picoblaze and the sequential Microblaze solutions are denoted as I_P and I_M. For example an improvement of $I_P = 100x$ means, the reconfigurable mesh algorithm performs 100 times faster than a single Picoblaze version. I avoid using the terms speedup for I_P and I_M since the underlying parallel and sequential algorithms are different. In the following, I present the four kernels and sketch the reconfigurable mesh algorithms. All results of this section a summarized in Figure 5.1.

Arithmetic: Sparse Matrix Multiplication   As an example arithmetic operation, I picked the reconfigurable mesh algorithm for sparse matrix multiplication (SMM) presented in [112]. The algorithm multiplies two matrices A and B of dimension $N \times N$ on an array of size $N \times N$ and is outlined in Algorithm 5.1. The elements $a_{ij} \in A$ and $b_{ij} \in B$ have to be preloaded to the corresponding nodes in the array.

The outer repeat-loop iterates over the maximum number of nonzero elements in a column, which is less or equal to k, the sparseness value. The inner forall-loops are executed only once but for all specified elements in parallel. Thus, forall-loops do not raise the complexity of the algorithm. In lines 19–37 a for-statement loops "all non-zero products" sequentially. As there are also at most k of these products per column, the runtime complexity of the algorithm is $\mathcal{O}(k^2)$ steps.

The practical realization of this reconfigurable mesh algorithm demonstrates the disparity between the algorithm formulation in pseudo code and the actual physical implementation. For example, the algorithm as described in [112] requires to "route the top-most nonzero p-element of column i to all nodes in row j", where j is the index given by one of the factors of p. Theoretically, this statement takes $\mathcal{O}(1)$ steps. The implementation as shown

---

Algorithm 5.1: Column-sparse matrix multiplication [112].

Data: Matrices $A_{(N,N)}$, $B_{(N,N)}$ with at most k nonzero elements per row stored on an $N \times N$ RMESH. PEs $P_{i,j}$ hold a_{ij} and b_{ij}

Result: $C_{(N,N)} = A \times B$ with c_{ij} stored at PE $P_{i,j}$

1 **repeat**
⎸   //Identify topmost nonzero element
2 ⎸ **forall** *PEs $P_{i,j}$* **pardo**
3 ⎸   **if** $a_{ij} \neq 0$ **then** Apply {N,S,W,E} pattern
4 ⎸   **else** Apply {NS,W,E} pattern
5 ⎸   **if** $i = 0$ **then** broadcast 1
6 ⎸   **else** read t from bus **if** $t = 1$ *AND* $a_{ij} \neq 0$ **then** Mark a_{ij} as topmost
7 ⎸ **parend**
⎸   //Broadcast the top-most nonzero A-element of column i
⎸   together with its row index to all PEs in row i
8 ⎸ **forall** *PEs $P_{i,j}$* **pardo**
9 ⎸   Apply {NS,W,E} pattern
10 ⎸   **if** $t = 1$ *AND* $a_{ij} \neq 0$ **then** Broadcast a_{ij} and i
11 ⎸   **else if** $i = j$ **then** Read $\hat{a}$ and $\hat{i}$
12 ⎸   Apply {N,S,WE} pattern
13 ⎸   **if** $i = j$ **then** Broadcast $\hat{a}$ and $\hat{i}$
14 ⎸   **else** Read $\hat{a}$ and $\hat{i}$
15 ⎸ **parend**
⎸   //Multiply received A-element with local B-element
16 ⎸ **forall** *PEs $P_{i,j}$* **pardo**
17 ⎸   Set $p_{ij} = \hat{a}b_{ij}$
18 ⎸ **parend**
19 ⎸ **for** *all non-zero products p* **do**
⎸   //Route the top-most nonzero p-element to the row
⎸   with the index given by the A-element
20 ⎸   **forall** *PEs $P_{i,j}$* **pardo**
21 ⎸   **if** $p_{ij} \neq 0$ **then** Apply {N,S,W,E} pattern
22 ⎸   **else** Apply {NS,W,E} pattern
23 ⎸   **if** $i = 0$ **then** broadcast 1
24 ⎸   **else** read t from bus
25 ⎸   **if** $t = 1$ *AND* $p_{(ij)} \neq 0$ **then** Mark p-element as topmost
26 ⎸   **parend**
27 ⎸   **forall** *PEs $P_{i,j}$* **pardo**
28 ⎸   Apply {NS,W,E} pattern
29 ⎸   **if** $t = 1$ *AND* $p_{(ij)} \neq 0$ **then** Broadcast $\hat{i}$
30 ⎸   **else** Read $\hat{i}$
31 ⎸   **if** $\hat{i} = i$ **then** Set $\hat{i} = 1$
32 ⎸   **else** Set $\hat{i} = 0$
33 ⎸   **if** $t = 1$ *AND* $p_{(ij)} \neq 0$ **then** Broadcast $p_{(ij)}$
34 ⎸   **else if** $\hat{i} = 1$ **then** Read s from bus and Set $c_{ij} = c_{ij} + s$
35 ⎸   **parend**
36 ⎸   Discard the top-most nonzero p-element
37 ⎸ **end**
38 ⎸ Discard the top-most nonzero A-element
39 **until** *All nonzero A-elements have been discarded*

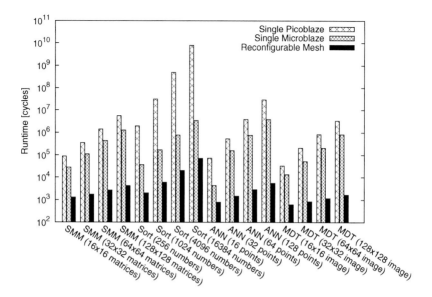

Figure 5.1: Runtime comparison of sequential and reconfigurable mesh solutions of the four case studies.

in 5.1 requires six column/row broadcasts to realize this step.

To fairly compare the parallel method with a sequential sparse matrix operation the sequential algorithm is highly optimized. It uses the Yale sparse matrix format [48] to store A and B. Furthermore, A is stored in a row-compressed and B in a column-compressed manner which allows for ideal access of parameters for the matrix-matrix multiplication kernel resulting in a very efficient execution of the matrix multiplication routine.

Results for the runtime comparison of reconfigurable mesh and sequential sparse matrix multiplications are shown in Table 5.1. In the reconfigurable mesh case, the runtime only increases from 33% to 58% when the problem size (and mesh size) is quadrupled. The numbers I_P and I_M show the runtime improvement of the reconfigurable mesh algorithm compared to the Picoblaze and Microblaze solutions, respectively.

Sorting and Selection: Schnorr and Shamir Several constant time sorting algorithms for reconfigurable meshes were proposed which sort N numbers

Matrix	Runtime [cycles]			Improvement	
	Picoblaze	Microblaze	R-Mesh	I_P	I_M
16×16	130662	27961	1312	67x	21x
32×32	359050	110137	1744	201x	63x
64×64	1434890	437305	2702	519x	162x
128×128	5736970	1274169	4262	1315x	299x

Table 5.1: Runtime comparison for sparse matrix multiplication algorithms.

on meshes of size $N \times N$ [82] [129] [126]. For sorting N^2 numbers on re-configurable meshes with N^2 processors, one can adopt optimal algorithms developed for general meshes. The sorting algorithm proposed by Schnorr and Shamir [143] sorts an $N \times N$ array in $3N + \mathcal{O}(N^{3/4})$ time. Algorithm 5.2 sketches the Schnorr and Shamir method. At the beginning, the processor array is divided into regular blocks of size $N^{3/4} \times N^{3/4}$; a horizontal (vertical) slice denotes a row (column) of blocks. In a first step, all blocks are sorted in a snake-like, row-major order in parallel. Second, the array performs a $N^{1/4}$-way unshuffle in all rows in parallel. That is, columns $iN^{1/4}$ ($0 \leq i < N^{3/4}$) are packed to the first $N^{1/4}$ columns of the array, columns $iN^{1/4} + 1$ are packed to the second $N^{1/4}$ columns, and so forth. Following this step, all blocks are again sorted in parallel. In Lines 9–17 several sorting steps are applied to different portions of the array. Finally, $N^{3/4}$ sorting steps have to be applied to the whole mesh to ensure that the array is sorted completely.

The counterpart sequential algorithm used for the single Microblaze system is quicksort. For the single Picoblaze case, bubblesort is applied because it matches most closely the processors limitation in performance and pro-grammability. For example, the build-in fixed size call-return stack makes divide & conquer algorithms like quicksort hard to implement. The compar-ison results in Table 5.2 show a very diverse runtime behavior of the three sorting algorithms. The $\mathcal{O}(N^2)$ bubblesort on the Picoblaze delivers bad results, even for smaller data sets. Compared to this, the $\mathcal{O}(N \log N)$ quick-sort on the Microblaze performs better by far, but is further improved by the reconfigurable mesh algorithm by factors ranging from 18 to 48.

Graph Algorithms: All Pairs Nearest Neighbor Given a set $S = \{p_i \mid 0 \leq i < N\}$ of points, the all pairs nearest neighbor (ANN) algorithm assigns to each p_i a sorted list $L_i = \langle p_j \rangle$ of the points $S' = S \setminus \{p_i\}$. ANN is a general case of the k-th nearest neighbor problem (KNN) because the lists L_i hold all $N - 1$

Algorithm 5.2: Schnorr and Shamir sorting algorithm [143].

Data: N^2 numbers, one per processor, distributed on a $N \times N$ reconfigurable mesh array
Result: N^2 numbers, sorted in snake-like row-major order

1 Partion the $N \times N$ reconfigurable mesh in $N^{1/2}$ blocks of size $N^{3/4} \times N^{3/4}$
2 **forall** *blocks b* **pardo**
3 | Sort b into snake-like row-major order
4 **forall** *rows i* **pardo**
5 | Perform a $N^{1/4}$-way unshuffle of row i.
6 **forall** *blocks b* **pardo**
7 | Sort b into snake-like row-major order
8 **forall** *colums i* **pardo**
9 | Sort i downwards
10 Partition the $N \times N$ reconfigurable mesh in vertical slices of size $N^{3/4} \times N$
11 **forall** *slices s* **pardo**
12 | Sort s into snake-like row-major order
13 **forall** *rows i* **pardo**
14 | **if** $i \mod 2 = 0$ **then**
15 | | Sort i in ascending order
16 | **else**
17 | | Sort i in descending order
18 Apply $N^{3/4}$ sorting steps to the array, indexed in snake-like row-major ordering

---

Input	Runtime [cycles]			Improvement	
	Picoblaze	Microblaze	R-Mesh	I_P	I_M
256	2624550	37143	2049	950x	18x
1024	41911014	171473	6065	5174x	28x
4096	501406144	775016	20049	25009x	39x
16384	8030380508	3432532	71825	111805x	48x

Table 5.2: Runtime comparison for sorting algorithms.

neighbors of p_i in ascending manner.

An ANN algorithm for general meshes is given in [115]. Constant time N-point ANN algorithms for $N \times N$ reconfigurable meshes are, for example, presented in [79]. The authors in [37] present an $\mathcal{O}(2^k)$ KNN algorithm for m points, stored according to their coordinates in the 2-D plan, on a $N \times N$ reconfigurable mesh.

As the architecture suffers from waiting time during communication phases, a different approach is used to solve the ANN problem. However, the algorithm, as presented in Algorithm 5.3, uses less broadcasts and performs better on the prototype than the $\mathcal{O}(1)$ algorithms mentioned above. Distance calculation is based on the Manhattan distance metric. In general, any other distance metric can be used for the algorithm.

At the beginning of Algorithm 5.3 N points $p_i = (x_i, y_i)$, $0 \leq i < N$ are stored in the first column of the $N \times N$ reconfigurable mesh. Each PE $P_{i,j}$ sets *colid* to the ID of the own column j. All PEs apply the $\{$N, S, WE$\}$ pattern to install row buses. The PEs on the first column broadcast their coordinates (x_i, y_i), all remaining nodes read (x_i, y_i). In a second step, all PEs apply the $\{$NS, W, E$\}$ pattern to install column buses. PEs on the diagonal broadcast (x_i, y_i) on column buses and all other processors read the coordinates in (x'_i, y'_i). At this point, each processor $P_{i,j}$ of the $N \times N$ reconfigurable mesh (with respect to the processors on the diagonal) stores two points, namely p_i and p_j. By calculating the (Manhattan) distance between p_i and p_j, the mesh computes an adjacency matrix of the points. In the final phase of the algorithm, the adjacency matrix is sorted inside the rows of the reconfigurable mesh in parallel. With every exchange step, also the parameter *colid* is exchanged which is used as a point-identifier. When the rows are sorted, processors $P_{i,j}$ holds the distance d from point p_i to the j-th nearest point p_{colid} of p_i.

I have implemented sequential ANN algorithms for Microblaze and Picoblaze processors. The algorithms first computes the distance matrix of the points and second sorts the rows of the matrix. By considering symmetry, the runtime of the sequential algorithm is optimized.

Table 5.3 compares runtime for the three ANN solutions. Note, that the problem size for this case study is $\sqrt{N}$ instead of N as for the other case studies. This is due to the fact, that the sequential algorithms (as well as the reconfigurable mesh algorithm) set up a distance table of size $N/2$ which is the basis for neighbor computation. Again, the reconfigurable mesh algorithm improves the runtime by several orders of magnitudes. The gain in improvement is even stronger compared to sparse matrix multiplication or sorting, regarding the Microblaze.

Image Algorithms: Manhattan Distance Transformation   For a given binary image, the distance transformation maps any pixel to the distance to the closest *foreground* or *black* pixel. Appropriate metrics for distance transformations are Euclidean or Manhattan distances. A comparative study of 2D Euclidean Distance Transformations (EDT) is presented in [60]. For the

---

Algorithm 5.3: All pairs nearest neighbors.

Data: N points $p_i = (x_i, y_i)$, $0 \le i < N$ distributed on an $N \times N$ reconfigurable mesh array. PEs $P_{i,0}$ hold coordinates (x_i, y_i) of point p_i

Result: PE $P_{i,j}$ stores the ID of the $j - th$ nearest point of $p_i = (x_i, y_i)$ in $colid$ as well as the corresponding Manhattan distance in d

1 **forall** *PEs* $P_{i,j}$ **pardo**
2 | Set $colid = j$
   //PEs on first column distribute coordinates on rows
3 Apply $\{N, S, WE\}$ pattern
4 **forall** *PEs* $P_{i,j}$ **pardo**
5 | **if** $j = 0$ **then** Broadcast (x_i, y_i) **else** Read (x_i', y_i')
   //Diagonal PEs distribute coordinates on columns
6 Apply $\{NS, W, E\}$ pattern
7 **forall** *PEs* $P_{i,j}$ **pardo**
8 | **if** $i = j$ **then** Broadcast (x_i, y_i)
9 | **else** Read (x_i', y_i')
   //Compute adjacency matrix
10 **forall** *PEs* $P_{i,j}$ **pardo**
11 | **if** $i = j$ **then** Set $d = MAXINT$
12 | **else** Set $d = |x - x'| + |y - y'|$
   //Sort adjacency matrix with node IDs
13 **forall** *Rows* i **pardo**
14 | Sort row i accosting to distance d by odd-even transposition sort. With every exchange operation exchange also $colid$.

Input	Runtime [cycles]			Improvement	
	Picoblaze	Microblaze	R-Mesh	I_P	I_M
16 points	100008	34319	788	93x	44x
32 points	717690	157997	1476	361x	107x
64 points	5406488	758385	2852	1353x	266x
128 points	41901656	3847395	5604	5256x	687x

Table 5.3: Runtime comparison for all pairs nearest neighbor algorithms.

general mesh and the reconfigurable mesh EDT algorithms are given in [52] and [19], respectively. The method used in this case study bases on [131] and is sketched in Algorithm 5.4. Figure 5.2 depicts three stages during an example EDT computation. To simplify the algorithm, Manhattan instead of Euclidean distances are applied.

Let a binary image be stored on a $N \times N$ reconfigurable mesh, one pixel per processor. In the first phase, all PEs $P_{i,j}$ determine the distance to the

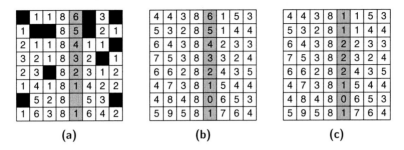

Figure 5.2: Three steps of the Manhattan distance transformation.

closest foreground pixel in the same column. To this end, PEs that store
a foreground pixel unfuse the bus and broadcast their *row_id i* first, to the
upper PEs and second to the lower PEs of the same column. If a PE holds
a background pixel, it sets the local switch pattern to {NS} and reads the
broadcasted *row_ids* from both, the upper and lower "black" PEs. With this
information, each PE can calculate its distance dc_i to the next foreground
pixel in its column (see Figure 5.2(a)). In the second phase, the rows of the
reconfigurable mesh apply a divide-and-conquer strategy to compute the final
Manhattan distances in parallel. First, the distance transformation values
for the PEs on the middle column $mc = \lceil N/2 \rceil$ are determined. Each PE
$P_{i,j}$ computes the minimal distance from a "foreground" PE in the same
column j to the middle PE on in the same row, which is $d_i = dc_i + |j - mc|$
(see Figure 5.2(b)). On each row, the PEs apply a standard $\mathcal{O}(\log \log N)$
reconfigurable mesh minimum algorithm to find the minimal d_i [159]. This
value is broadcasted on the row bus and stored as final result d by the PEs in
column mc (see Figure 5.2(c)). When the nodes on the middle column know
their final distance transformation results, the current mesh can be divided
into two equal size (except for one column) sub-meshes of size $N \times (N/2)$
and the distance transformation values for the two middle colums of the sub-
meshes can be computed in parallel. After $\log N$ iterations of phase two, the
recursion terminates and each PE holds the result in d.

Distance transformation algorithms are very dependent on the underlying
distance metric. In case of the Manhattan distance, the sequential 2D algorithm is quite straightforward. During a first pass, all rows of the image
are passed through in left to right and right to left directions, to determine
for each background pixel the minimal distance to a foreground pixel in the
same row. An analogue 2-way pass is then executed on the columns of the

---

Algorithm 5.4: Manhattan distance transformation.

Data: A binary image stored on a $N \times N$ reconfigurable mesh, one pixel per
PE

Result: PE $P_{i,j}$ stores the Manhattan distance to the closest foreground
pixel in d

//Broadcast foreground pixel positions on columns, upwards

1 **forall** *PEs* $P_{i,j}$ **pardo**

2   **if** $P_{i,j}$ *is foreground pixel* **then** Apply {N} pattern and broadcast i

3   **else** Apply {NS,W,E} pattern and read dc_l

//Broadcast foreground pixel positions on columns,
downwards

4 **forall** *PEs* $P_{i,j}$ **pardo**

5   **if** $P_{i,j}$ *is foreground pixel* **then** Apply {S} pattern and broadcast i)

6   **else** Apply {NS,W,E} pattern and read dc_u. Set $dc_i = |dc_l - dc_u|$

7 set_distance$((0, N))$

8 **function** set_distance (l, r) **is**

9   **forall** *PEs* $\{P_{i,j} | l \leq j \leq r\}$ **pardo**

10   Set $mc = l + \lceil (r - l)/2 \rceil$

11   **if** $mc = 1$ **then return**

12   Set $d_i = dc_i + |j - mc|$

13   **forall** *Rows* k **pardo**

       //Connect PEs $\{P_{k,j} | l \leq j \leq r\}$ on a shared sub-bus

14   **if** $j = l$ **then** Apply {E} pattern

15   **else if** $j = r$ **then** Apply {W} pattern

16   **else if** $l < j < r$ **then** Apply {N,S,WE} pattern

17   Find minimal d_i on all sub-buses

18   **forall** *PEs* $\{P_{i,j} | l \leq j \leq r\}$ **pardo**

19   **if** d_i *is minimum* **then** broadcast d_i

20   **else if** $j=mc$ **then** read d from bus

21   Start **set_distance**$((l, mc))$ and **set_distance**$((mc, r))$ in parallel

---

image. In this run, the minimum of the distance to a foreground pixel on
the same row and the precomputed distance for the rows is taken as distance
value for a background pixel.

Table 5.4 shows the runtime results for the sequential algorithm compared
to the reconfigurable mesh version. The improvement results for this case
study a right in the line with the SMM and ANN cases. Compared to one
Microblaze, a reconfigurable mesh with 128×128 PEs operates 488 times
faster.

Image	Runtime [cycles]			Improvement	
	Picoblaze	Microblaze	R-Mesh	I_P	I_M
16×16	58868	13346	620	53x	22x
32×32	232364	52701	850	245x	62x
64×64	1123436	207767	1182	703x	176x
128×128	3681836	828198	1696	1956x	488x

Table 5.4: Runtime comparison for Manhattan distance transformation algorithms.

5.1.2 Microblaze Case Study

Matrix multiplication serves as an application to study the Microblaze based many-core architecture. I compare three different implementations of matrix multiplication algorithms for single cores, shared memory multi-cores and, finally, for the mesh-based processor array utilizing the lightweight reconfigurable mesh interconnect.

The three different matrix multiplication algorithms are:

- As a single core reference algorithm, the classical $\mathcal{O}(n^3)$ "paper and pencil" method for matrix multiplication is applied and executed on the master node of the array.

- In the shared memory algorithm which runs on $k = 1 \ldots 6$ memory nodes of the array, each processor computes N/k rows of the $N \times M$ result matrix. As multiple processors never perform write operations to the same shared memory locations or read modified data, there is no need for synchronization inside the matrix multiplication kernel.

- The mesh matrix multiplication algorithm distributes the matrices over the processor array to employ all available cores and utilizes the reconfigurable mesh based interconnection network for communication. The algorithm starts with an initialization phase where all nodes form a global bus and the master node broadcasts the mesh dimensions and the matrix size. The actual matrix multiplication algorithm is then executed on the specified array size; the local block size can be computed based on the mesh dimensions and the matrix size. Possibly unused processors remain spare.

Algorithm 5.5 presents the mesh-based parallel matrix multiplication in more detail. The algorithm assumes, that the parameters n, m, p and q have

---

Algorithm 5.5: Blockwise parallel matrix multiplication.

Data: Matrices $A \in \mathbb{R}^{n,s}$ and $B \in \mathbb{R}^{s,m}$
Result: Multiply $C = AB$ on a $p \times q$ array of nodes

1 **swconf(** WE **)**
2 **#if** *Memory node of row k*
3 $\quad$| $\quad$ Broadcasts **submatrix(** $A, \frac{k \cdot n}{p}, \frac{(k+1) \cdot n}{p}, 0, s$ **)** on local bus
4 **#elsif** *Worker node*
5 $\quad$| $\quad$ Read data from bus and store it local scratchpad as $\hat{A} \in \mathbb{R}^{\frac{n}{p},s}$
6 **#endif**
7 **#if** *Memory node of row k*
8 $\quad$| $\quad$ Broadcasts **submatrix(** $B, \frac{k \cdot s}{q}, \frac{(k+1) \cdot s}{q}, 0, m$ **)** on local bus
9 **#elsif** *Worker node*
10 $\quad$| $\quad$ Read data from bus and store it local scratchpad as $\hat{B} \in \mathbb{R}^{\frac{s}{p},m}$
11 **#endif**
12 **sync**
13 **swconf(** NS **)**
14 **all** *Nodes on col j* **in parallel do**
15 $\quad$| $\quad T \in \mathbb{R}^{\frac{s}{p},\frac{m}{q}}$ $\leftarrow$ **submatrix(** $B, 0, \frac{s}{p}, \frac{j \cdot m}{q}, \frac{(j+1) \cdot m}{q}$ **)**
16 **end**
17 **for** $0 \leq i < p$ **do**
18 $\quad$| $\quad$ **all** *Columns* **in parallel do**
19 $\quad$| $\quad$| $\quad$ **#if** *Node is located on row i*
20 $\quad$| $\quad$| $\quad$| $\quad$ Broadcast T on local bus segment.
21 $\quad$| $\quad$| $\quad$ **#elsif** *Worker node*
22 $\quad$| $\quad$| $\quad$| $\quad$ Read T from bus.
23 $\quad$| $\quad$| $\quad$ **#endif**
24 $\quad$| $\quad$| $\quad \left(\bar{b}_{i \cdot \frac{m}{q} + x, y} \right) \leftarrow (t_{x,y}), \ \bar{B} \in \mathbb{R}^{s, \frac{m}{q}}$
25 $\quad$| $\quad$ **end**
26 $\quad$| $\quad$ **sync**
27 **end**
28 Multiply $\hat{C} \leftarrow \hat{A}\bar{B}, \ \hat{C} \in \mathbb{R}^{\frac{n}{p},\frac{m}{q}}$
29 **sync**
30 **swconf(** WE **)**
31 **#if** *memory node of row i*
32 $\quad$| $\quad$ Write back local block $\hat{C}$ of C to external memory
33 **#endif**
34 **sync**
35 **for** $1 \leq j < q$ **do**
36 $\quad$| $\quad$ **all** *Rows* **in parallel do**
37 $\quad$| $\quad$| $\quad$ **#if** *j-th processor in row*
38 $\quad$| $\quad$| $\quad$| $\quad$ Broadcast local block $\hat{C}$ on local bus
39 $\quad$| $\quad$| $\quad$ **#elsif** *memory node*
40 $\quad$| $\quad$| $\quad$| $\quad$ Read block $\hat{C}$ from bus and write back to external memory
41 $\quad$| $\quad$| $\quad$ **#endif**
42 $\quad$| $\quad$ **end**
43 $\quad$| $\quad$ **sync**
44 **end**
45 **function** submatrix $(M, r0, r1, c0, c1)$ **is**
46 $\quad$| $\quad \hat{M} \leftarrow (m_{x,y}), \ r0 \leq x < r1, \ c0 \leq y < c1$
47 $\quad$| $\quad$ **return** $\hat{M} \in \mathbb{R}^{r1-r0,c1-c0}$
48

---

already been distributed on the array. At the beginning, the network is reconfigured to install row buses. The active memory nodes then read the multiplicands A and B from memory and scatter them over the $p \times q$ array of processors. After two broadcast phases of the memory nodes, the array stores horizontal stripes of A and B. As the individual nodes have to multiply rows of A with columns of B, matrix B is transposed inside the columns of the array. For this purpose, the programs are synchronized by calling a barrier, reconfigure the network to install column buses and execute a blockwise transposition of B. After this step, each processor stores horizontal stripes of A and vertical stripes of B and has therefore all information to compute a partial result matrix of size $n/p \times m/q$. For writing back the result matrix C to memory, the processor array installs row buses. Again, the memory nodes manage the write back of all sub-matrices to external memory.

Scaling the Mesh Size To study how the matrix multiplication scales with the number of utilized processors, Algorithm 5.5 is executed on varying portions of the 6×6 Microblaze reconfigurable mesh many-core. Table 5.5 shows the runtime comparison for a 12×12 matrix multiplication on the single core, shared memory multi-core, and mesh-based array. Column *Size* denotes the size of the (sub-) mesh of utilized PEs, column *Block* mentions the size of the sub-matrix for which the used PEs compute the multiplication result, column *T* lists the measured runtime in cycles, and column *Mem* specifies the data location. In the case of the single core reference implementation all data is located in local scratchpad (BRAM) allowing for optimal memory access. When using the shared memory or the mesh implementation all source and target matrices are located in external memory. The shared memory implementation can use cached or uncached access to external memory, while the mesh implementation relies on cached accesses. The two right-most columns present the absolute runtime improvement factor over the single core implementation, $I(abs)$, and the relative improvement concerning the utilized number of cores, $I(rel) = I(abs)/\#cores$.

Compared to the single core algorithm, the shared memory algorithm incurs some overhead since it has to take dynamic decisions. To evaluate this overhead, the shared memory algorithm is applied to a single core, denoted as "1×1" in Table 5.5. When using caches, the slowdown is limited and amounts to 0.95x compared to the single core case. Lines 4–5 of Table 5.5 show the runtime improvement for the shared memory implementation. A six core shared memory system can improve the multiplication performance by 5.45x. Lines 6–12 of Table 5.5 show the runtime improvements for the

Size	Block	T[cycles]	Mem	$I(abs)$	$I(rel)$
Single core					
1	12×12	123772	BRAM	1	1
1×1	12×12	190817	uncached	0.65	0.65
1×1	12×12	130239	cached	0.95	0.95
Shared memory					
6×1	2×12	47180	uncached	2.72	0.45
6×1	2×12	26137	cached	5.45	0.91
Reconfigurable mesh					
6×6	2×2	6263	cached	19.76	0.55
6×4	2×3	7446	cached	16.62	0.69
4×6	3×2	8572	cached	14.44	0.60
6×3	2×4	8797	cached	14.07	0.78
3×6	4×2	10886	cached	11.37	0.63
6×2	2×6	11189	cached	11.06	0.92
2×6	6×2	15540	cached	7.96	0.66

Table 5.5: Runtime comparison for 12×12 matrix multiplication.

mesh implementation on several architectural configurations. The 6×6 solution utilizes all 36 cores, a 6×3 mesh uses the complete first 3 columns, and a 3×6 mesh utilizes the 18 cores on the upper three rows of the processor array. I have measured improvement factors ranging from 19.76x when all cores are used to 7.96x when only two rows of the mesh are utilized. Generally, meshes with more memory nodes are faster since they benefit from a higher bandwidth to external memory. Even in terms of relative improvement $I(rel)$, one reconfigurable mesh solution (0.92 for the 6×2 configuration) comes close to the single core efficiency of 0.95 and even beats the best shared memory solution.

All runtime measurements stated in Table 5.5 are for homogeneous arrays where the multiplications are emulated in software. For the heterogeneous array, i.e., the nodes on the first three columns including the master and all memory nodes support hardware multiplication, the improvement factors for the mesh algorithm decreases to 3.25x–1.74x, depending on the array size. However, in this case also the improvement factor for the shared memory algorithm decreases to 1.15x if caches are used and to 0.84x if caches are turned off.

Scaling the Problem Size   To study the scalability with problem size, I compare the three matrix multiplication implementations for matrix sizes of up to 384×384. Figure 5.3 shows the absolute and relative improvement factors for the 6-core shared memory and 36-core mesh algorithms over the single core algorithm with and without hardware multiplication support. Since the worker nodes in the many-core prototype have a rather limited amount of local memory (4kB scratchpad RAM for instructions and data), only a few rows and columns of the multiplicand matrices can be stored locally. Therefore, each of the Figures 5.3(a)–(d) displays two curves for the mesh implementation. The first curve represents data measured on a mesh implementation for matrix sizes up to 30×30. The second curve is for larger matrix sizes which requires us to emulate a larger local RAM. The emulation changes the mesh matrix multiplication code to simply re-use (overwrite) the same memory locations for different blocks of the matrices. The additional code needed for the emulation forms an overhead resulting in a rather conservative estimation of the runtime.

Figures 5.3(a) and 5.3(c) show the absolute and relative improvements, respectively, for the heterogeneous array. The runtime improvements for the 6-core shared memory implementation are almost constant over the matrix size and are in the range of 1.23x to 1.76x for *I(abs)* and between 0.2 and 0.3 for *I(rel)* compared to a single core. The improvement for the 36-core mesh implementation, however, increases with the problem size until the communication effort within the array becomes negligible. For a matrix size of 384×384 the absolute runtime improvement is 14.08x. In terms of relative improvement factors, the mesh algorithm beats the shared memory algorithm for matrix sizes larger than 30×30. Generally, the relative improvement factors are rather low for the heterogeneous array since the single core reference enjoys the fastest memory access and a hardware multiplier.

Figures 5.3(b) and 5.3(d) quantify the absolute and relative improvements, respectively, for the homogeneous array where multiplication is emulated in software on all nodes. Compared to the heterogeneous array, the absolute and relative improvement factors are higher. Again, the absolute improvement for the 6-core shared memory is rather constant and varies between 5.07x and 5.73x. The mesh algorithm requires larger problem sizes to saturate the improvement factor which peaks at 36.52x. In terms of relative improvement factors, the mesh starts to beat the shared memory implementation at smaller problem sizes in comparison to the heterogeneous array. This is expected since also the memory nodes have to emulate multiplications in software. For some specific problem sizes, the mesh reveals relative improvement factors larger than one, which are effects of the different algorithms used for matrix multiplication.

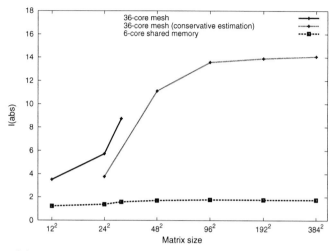

(a) Absolute improvement factor for the heterogeneous array

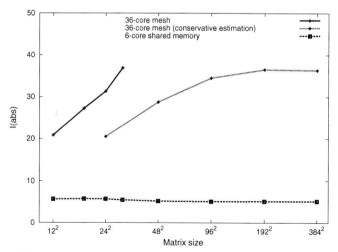

(b) Absolute improvement factor for the homogeneous array

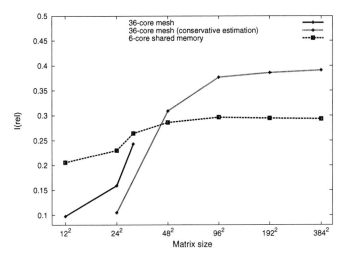

(c) Relative improvement factor for the heterogeneous array

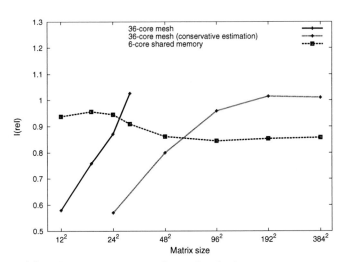

(d) Relative improvement factor for the homogeneous array

Figure 5.3: Improvements for shared memory and mesh-bases matrix multiplication implementations compared to the single core implementation.

5.2 Achieving Fault-Tolerance

A fault-tolerant system must be able to continue operation, even if some of the systems' components are faulty. In the context of the massively parallel reconfigurable mesh architecture, fault tolerance techniques on the architectural and algorithmic level are of particular interest. A specific problem is to identify and mask faulty nodes in the reconfigurable mesh and form a healthy sub-mesh out of the remaining operational nodes. This section focuses on methods for self-testing a reconfigurable mesh to identify permanent faults on processors. Detection and reaction on dynamic failures during algorithm execution is much more involved. Fault tolerance aspects of the reconfigurable mesh are, for example, discussed in [59].

A basic method for identifying a healthy sub-mesh in a reconfigurable mesh with faulty nodes works as follows:

1. Configure row buses. The left-most nodes broadcast a '1' on the bus, the other nodes read the bus.

2. The right-most nodes broadcast a '1' on the bus, the other nodes read the bus. A node that either receives two '1' or is an intact right/left boundary node, marks itself as *row-complete*.

3. The mesh is reconfigured to install column buses and the steps 1 and 2 are repeated on the columns. Nodes that either receive two '1' or are intact upper/lower boundary nodes mark themselves as *column-complete*.

4. Nodes marked as both *row-complete* and *column-complete* build up a healthy sub-mesh. Nodes marked only as *row-complete* or *column-complete* are turned into routing nodes and apply the {WE, N, S} or {NS, W, E} communication pattern, respectively. Intact nodes that are neither *row-complete* nor *column-complete* do not fuse any of their ports.

As an example, Figure 5.4(a) shows a 5×5 reconfigurable mesh with two faulty nodes. After applying the self testing algorithm the mesh reorganizes to a healthy 3×3 sub-mesh shown in Figure 5.4(b). Generally, for an $N \times M$ reconfigurable mesh with k faulty nodes, the method keeps at least $NM - k(N + M - k)$ operational nodes in the reorganized healthy mesh. In the example of Figure 5.4 with $N = M = 5$ and $k = 2$, only 9 out of 25 nodes remain fully operational. For a reconfigurable mesh of size 100×100 and 5 faulty nodes, the reasonable number of at least $100^2 - 5(200 - 5) = 9025$ nodes stay intact.

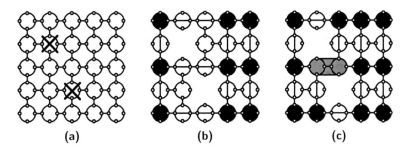

Figure 5.4: Healthy sub-mesh identification: Faulty 5 × 5 reconfigurable mesh(a) healthy 3 × 3 sub-mesh (b) and healthy 3 × 4 sub-mesh with one pair-wise complete column (c).

Figure 5.4(c) shows an optimized method for installing a healthy sub-mesh. The algorithm also identifies so-called pair-wise complete rows or columns. In the example, columns 1 and 2 are incomplete, but together they build a pair-wise complete column. The two gray nodes in the third row form a super node that can simulate a complete column by proper switch settings. For example, the switch pattern {NS,W,E} is simulated by the two patterns {SE,N,W} for node (2,1) and {NW,S,E} for node (2,2). This specific technique is only applicable to the RMESH model, as a super node can not simulate double-bus patterns such as {NW,SE} or {NS,WE}.

Listing 5.1 shows an implementation of the basic healthy sub-mesh identification algorithm in ARMLang. The dimensions of the reconfigurable mesh are specified in brackets after the program name. In the example, the algorithm will be executed on a 16 × 16 mesh. After all nodes have configured the {WE,N,S} pattern, the right-most node of each row broadcasts its '1'. All other nodes wait for WIDTH cycles, i.e., 16 cycles, before they read the bus. The right-most processors broadcast a '1' on the row buses and all nodes check whether they are *row-complete*. The same process is repeated for the columns and the nodes check whether they are *column-complete*. Finally, depending on row- and column-completeness the nodes configure their switches accordingly.

Figure 5.5 displays a simulation screen shot showing a 16 × 16 reconfigurable mesh including 4 faulty nodes with processors IDs 34, 134, 186 and 228. Faultiness of the nodes was carried out by erasing the nodes program. The figure also indicates the healthy sub-mesh identified by the *findhealthysub-mesh* algorithm of Listing 5.1. The sub-mesh can be formed by executing a

```
PROGRAM findhealthysubmesh(16:16);
DECLARE
  a : INTEGER; b : INTEGER; rowc : INTEGER;
  columnc : INTEGER; healthy : INTEGER
BEGIN
  healthy := 0;
  //check rows
  SWITCH WE
  a := 1; b := 1;
  WHERE PID%WIDTH==0 DO WRITE(a)
  ELSEWHERE WAIT(WIDTH); READ(a) END;
  WHERE (PID%WIDTH)==(WIDTH-1) DO WRITE(b)
  ELSEWHERE WAIT(WIDTH); READ(b) END;
  rowc := 0;
  IF (a==1) THEN
    IF (b==1) THEN rowc := 1 END
  END;
  //check columns
  a := 1; b := 1;
  SWITCH NS;
  WHERE PID/WIDTH==0 DO WRITE(a)
  ELSEWHERE WAIT(HEIGHT); READ(a) END;
  WHERE PID/WIDTH==(HEIGHT-1) DO WRITE(b)
  ELSEWHERE WAIT(HEIGHT); READ(b) END;
  columnc := 0;
  IF (a==1) THEN
    IF (b==1) THEN columnc := 1 END
  END;
  //set flags
  IF (rowc==1) THEN
    IF columnc == 1 THEN
      healthy := 1;
      SWITCH VOID
    ELSE SWITCH WE
    END
  ELSE
    IF columnc == 1 THEN SWITCH NS END
  END
END.
```

Listing 5.1: Healthy submesh identification in ARMLang.

sequence of 80 clock cycles assuming the theoretical constant time broadcast model or in 144 cycles using FPGA prototype.

5.3 HV-RN Self-Simulation

For a practical implementation, the optimality of a self simulation technique, as depicted in Section 2.2.5, is of limited significance. In a real architec-

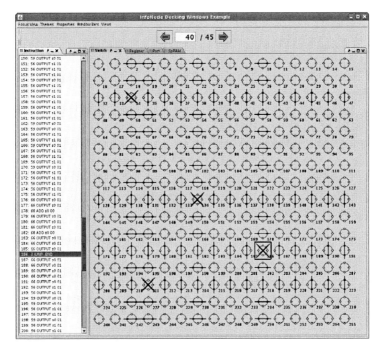

Figure 5.5: Simulation of the healthy sub-mesh identification algorithm in listing 5.1.

ture, each communication step of the theoretical model takes a number of clock cycles depending on the array size. If an algorithm's ratio of computation to communication cycles is low, a self simulation technique can lead to substantial overhead. A novel challenge for practical reconfigurable mesh architectures is the development of new mapping techniques which reduce the simulation overhead.

As one example for demonstrating the HV-RN self-simulation technique I have implemented an algorithm that embeds a binary tree into the reconfigurable mesh in the language ARMLang (see A.4 for details). This algorithm can be applied to various problems, e.g., addition in the present example. The algorithm starts with summing up all values on single rows of the array. Therefore, neighboring elements of the rows are connected to form pairs of processors. The left-most processor of each sub-bus broadcasts its value, the right-most processor reads the bus and adds the fetched value to its locally

95

stored number. Then, processors that have written onto the bus apply the $\{\mathtt{WE},\mathtt{N},\mathtt{S}\}$ pattern and will no longer take place in the computation. After $\log_2 N$ of such steps, the sum of the N values of a row is stored in the processor of the first column. In a second phase the processors in the first column sum up their partial results in the same manner. Eventually, the top-left processor contains the overall result.

Three different architectures have been used to compute the sum of $2^{12} = 4096$ integers. Table 5.6 shows the comparison of the runtimes. On a single Microblaze processor the execution of a program for adding all 2^{12} elements of a two-dimensional array stored in local memory, compiled with ggc and best optimization, takes 24696 cycles. A 64×64 instance of the Picoblaze many-core using the proposed reconfigurable mesh algorithm would need 528 steps, resulting in a speedup of 46.8 compared to the single processor solution. This result has been obtained using the cycle-accurate simulator.

On the FPGA implementation of a 16×16 Picoblaze many-core instance, a self simulation technique is required to compute the algorithm. As the binary tree embedding uses only the patterns $\{\mathtt{NS},\mathtt{W},\mathtt{E}\}$ and $\{\mathtt{WE},\mathtt{N},\mathtt{S}\}$, the discussed self simulation technique for the HV-RN model could be used to map the "virtual" 64×64 to the 16×16 array of Picoblaze processors. However, applying this general technique to the problem of adding numbers leads to a huge runtime overhead. Instead, one can sum up all 16 elements of a 4×4 sub-mesh on a physical node directly because the addition is an associative binary operation.

This results in a much more efficient self simulation approach which, on the 16×16 reconfigurable mesh instance, takes only 308 clock cycles corresponding to a speedup of 80.2 compared to the Microblaze.

A surprising result is that the scaling simulation on the 16×16 mesh is even faster than the original algorithm performed on a large 64×64 system. This is due to the fact that the problem-specific self simulation approach increases the amount of computation per node dramatically in relation to the communication. This experiment makes clear that for practical reconfigurable mesh implementations, the native mesh size is not necessarily optimal. A characterization of algorithms according to their ratio between computation cycles and communication cycles on a real architecture, and the identification of the optimal mesh size in dependence of this ratio is desirable.

For a second example of self simulation I review the sorting problem again. An elementary algorithm for sorting two-dimensional arrays is shear-sort [142]. On an $N \times N$ array of processors shear-sort runs in $\log(N)$ rounds. In each round, first the rows and second the columns of the array a sorted

	Datasize	Runtime [cycles]	Speedup
Microblaze	2^{12}	24696	1.0
64x64 R-Mesh	2^{12}	528	46.8
16x16 R-Mesh	2^{12}	308	80.2

Table 5.6: Runtime and speedup results for addition of 2^{12} numbers on different architectures

separately in parallel. Shear-sort has a time complexity of $\Theta(N \log(N))$ and is thus not optimal regarding the area-time complexity criterion [155]. However, due to its simplicity – the ARMLang implementation, for example, needs only 116 lines of code – the general shear-sort algorithm can be extended to run in self-simulation mode with reasonable effort. As shear-sort only affords communication patterns that are supported by the HV-RN model, the HV-RN self-simulation strategy as depicted in Section 2.2.5 can be applied. By using contraction mapping, an $N/P \times N/P$ sub-mesh of the original $N \times N$ reconfigurable mesh is mapped to each processor of the $P \times P$ array. In each algorithm step, processor $S(i,j)$ simulates the computation phases of each node of the simulated sub-mesh. In the following communication phase, each row and column broadcast is simulated in sequence.

First, I analyzed the general shear-sort algorithm. Sorting 256 numbers on a 16×16 array consumes 5232 cycles, including 1134 cycles for data I/O. For a custom shear-sort self-simulation, a 2×2 sub-mesh bas mapped to each PE of the 256-core Picoblaze array. This algorithm is able to sort 1024 values on a 16×16 array in 24852 cycles. As the size of the simulated sub-mesh is a matter of parameters and only bounded by the processors local memory, this sorting routine is perfectly scalable on a fixed size mesh. As the results indicate, the overhead for self-simulation is limited: Sorting a four times larger array consumes $4.75x$ cycles on a same size reconfigurable mesh.

5.4 Chapter Conclusion

I have provided numerous results for reconfigurable mesh based many-cores established in prior chapters. Runtime experiments show that pure reconfigurable mesh algorithms can beat sequential solutions by several orders of magnitude. The results are drawn form runtime measurements of FPGA prototypes as well as cycle-accurate simulations which both comprise the overhead of multi-cycle communication delays. For a matrix-multiplication case study a many-core with reconfigurable mesh interconnect could beat a shared memory 6-core system even in terms of efficiency. The experiments expose, that for suitable applications the reconfigurable mesh system can almost completely compensate the communication costs and reaches an N-fold speedup for an N-core system compared to a sequential solution. To make the many-core architecture more robust against faulty nodes, a self-test method is presented and implemented for the Picoblaze mesh variant. The algorithm involves a very limited overhead and consumes just 4 row/column broadcasts to determine healthy cores and setup an operative sub-mesh. To tackle the issue of scalability, I have implemented an optimal self-simulation technique for HV-RN reconfigurable meshes in ARMLang. However, as self-simulation methods do not reduce broadcast steps and even increase communication costs, I propose to rather modify the algorithm than to apply a general self-simulation. To this end, I demonstrate how reconfigurable mesh algorithms can be scaled efficiently. In one example, the custom self-simulation could even reduce runtime compared to a larger size mesh computing the very same problem.

CHAPTER 6

A Hybrid Interconnect for Many-Cores

The previous chapters present an architecture and programming tool flow for
FPGA many-cores inspired by the reconfigurable mesh model of computation.
Technically, only the communication network sticks to the reconfigurable
mesh model. The array of PEs and the programming flow could generally be
used for different programming models. However, the reconfigurable mesh
network is not well suited for general communication. Although generality
could be enforced – for example, arbitrary one-to-one messages could be
managed by configuring the network to install a globally shared bus and by
handling the send requests sequentially – the communication would be fairly
inefficient.

For supporting a broader class of applications, the communication capabilities of the many-core should be extended. A general concept for communication in large-scale Systems-on-Chip is known as Network-on-Chip (NoC). The
main idea behind NoCs is to connect several cores through an universal communication network that can handle the transport of messages autonomously.
The cores have a single access point to the network instead of dedicated links
to some other nodes. To initiate a communication, the core has to wrap its
message into packets, i.e., the payload data has to be equipped with control
information.

In the following, I present the design and implementation of a packet-switched
NoC. Results regarding the used resources are given in Section 6.2. The NoC
and the reconfigurable mesh network can be combined to form a hybrid

communication infrastructure. Section 6.3 evaluates the hybrid interconnect by benchmarking communication primitives and by a Jacobi method case study.

6.1 Wormhole Routed Packet-Switched NoC

A reconfigurable mesh network enables the Microblaze based many-core to exploit algorithms developed for the reconfigurable mesh programming model. The network is also efficient for simulating other topologies, like trees or pyramid. All this applications have in common, that the communication requirements fit well to the network's architecture. But there are also applications which rely on communication patterns that can not efficiently implemented with a reconfigurable mesh based interconnect. To this end, an additional packet-switched network extends the communication capabilities of the many-core. A packet-switched network allows for more flexible communication patterns, as any node can send messages to any other node at any time. Guerrier and Greiner [70], Dally and Towles [44] as well as Benini and DeMicheli [28] coined the term Network-on-Chip or, for short NoC[1] for a packet based interconnect among multiple cores on a single die. NoCs are proposed to replace design-specific global on-chip wires and shared bus communication infrastructures which are shown to be not well scalable. Today, NoCs are widely accepted to be the most promising interconnect for large scale SoC and multi-core architectures. The number of NoC related publications has grown dramatically in the last years. While the NoC's strength is generality, it is weaker than the reconfigurable mesh in terms of resource utilization and broadcast or multicast capabilities.

Architectural aspects of NoCs like interconnect topologies, routing algorithms or flow control can be adopted from well-studied off-die networks. Researchers commonly recommend a layered design methodology for NoCs similar to the OSI model for general computer networks. In their survey [30] Bjerregaard and Mahadevan partition the spectrum of NoC research into the four areas i) system level, ii) network adapters, iii) network and iv) link level. The *system level* encompasses applications and the systems architecture in general, most details about the network implementation are not relevant at this level. For the NoC architecture presented in this thesis, software aspects of the system level are covered in Section 4.3 and hardware architectures are discussed in Section 3.4. The *network adapter* or *network interface* decouples the cores from the network and handles end-to-end flow control of messages.

---

[1] In their pioneering papers, Guerrier/Greiner and Dally/Towles use the term "on-chip network". In further research the term network-on-chip (NoC) has been established.

Other architectural aspects are covered by the *network* layer and include network topology, protocol (routing, switching, control schemes), flow control (deadlock avoidance, virtual channels, buffering), quality of service and features (error correction, broadcast/multicast/narrowcast, virtual wires). At the lowest abstraction level, the *link level* deals with encoding and synchronization issues of data flits (flow control units). As being most relevant for the NoC's architecture, levels ii) and iii) of the layered model are detailed below. Figure 6.1 sketches the router architecture for the proposed NoC.

Network interface and packet format: The proposed many-core is targeted to data-parallel applications and thus, it greatly benefits from a tight coupling of PEs and the network. To support such a tight coupling, all of the network interfaces (barrier net, reconfigurable mesh and NoC) are connected to a fast simplex link port of the Microblaze core. For starting a message transfer, the Microblaze core issues the packet as a sequence of 32-bit data words to the FSL interface. As the build-in put instructions typically consume only a single cycle per data word, which makes the transfer of register contents to the FSL link rather efficient. There is no burst mode available, i.e., each chunk of data has to be fetched from memory and stored to a register by the processor before sending to the NoC. However, as the many-core array operates at a relatively fine-grained level where parallel constituents of an application basically communicate operands, this is not a profound limitation.

The FIFO based network interface can be used to decouple the cores and the networks clock domains by configuring the FSL interfaces to operate in an asynchronous mode. As the routers data paths are relatively simple and wires are short, the network can normally be clocked faster than the cores. Section 3.4.2 presents details on the achieved clock frequencies for the FPGA many-core prototypes.

Each message starts with a packet header, delivered with the first 32-bit word of a transaction. The first header byte contains the target node's position, the second byte the sender node's position in the processor array. To simplify route computation, processor addresses are coded by (x, y) positions. Thus, the maximum array size is $2^4 \times 2^4$. The third byte specifies the message length in 32-bit words including the header. The last byte of the header is currently unused and might later serve for specifying packet types or for hierarchical routing if more than 256 nodes need to be addressed in subsequent implementations.

Since wormhole routing is used, a message must be completely available before sending. Otherwise, the network would interpret gaps in the transmission

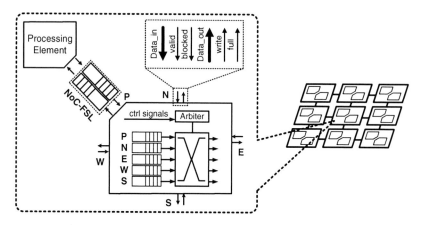

Figure 6.1: Router Architecture for the proposed NoC.

(which can occur when the NoC sends data packets faster than the processor can deliver them) as valid data. While one could easily extend the datapath with a valid signal to indicate valid data, this might heavily extend the length of a packet stream and thus increase the network load. The proposed NoC architecture ensures message continuity by buffering the complete packet in the outgoing FIFO of the FSL interface. I have developed network interface modules, called NoC-FSL in Figure 6.1, which are based on the Xilinx FSL cores. To let the FIFO interface handle the packet transmission, the internal (synchronous and asynchronous) FSL cores were extended to output their current level. As the packet length is enclosed in the header, the network interface can start issuing the data to the NoC when all words of the packet are buffered. Once the packet is passed to the NoC, each router in the path from source to target node induces a best case latency of exactly two cycles. A single control line extends the data path to mark the packet's tail flit. After forwarding a tail flit, the arbiter gets released and, potentially, the transmission of a waiting packet can be started.

The data width of the network is intended to be configurable at a byte-wise granularity. As a consequence, 32-bit data words must be split in several flits and sequentially forwarded, if the networks data width is smaller than the Microblaze's word size. The current implementation uses a data width of 8-bit, i.e., each data word is transmitted as a sequence of four bytes. The sequencing and reconstruction of data words is handles automatically by the NoC-FSL interface modules.

Topology: As for the reconfigurable mesh based network, a two-dimensional mesh topology is used for the NoC. This design consideration has been tied down, because a mesh topology has lower hardware requirements than other 2D interconnect topologies. In a torus, for example, a cyclic waiting of packets can occur when using dimension order routing. To prevent such deadlock situations, it is sufficient to extend the routers with virtual channels. Albeit a torus topology and virtual channel routers might increase the performance of the NoC, the required resources for implementing this features would increase the router's complexity significantly, resulting in higher area and power demands.

Routing: As routing strategy, XY-routing (2D dimension-order routing) is applied, which is a deadlock and livelock avoiding deterministic routing algorithm for two-dimensional meshes. XY-routing incurs minimal hardware cost and is shown to deliver the best power-per-throughput ratio compared to other (non virtual channel) alternatives such as odd-even routing and negative first turn routing [116]. As the packet header format encodes target node addresses by (x, y)-positions, the routing decisions can be computed very efficiently.

Ports: Incoming channels from adjacent routers and from the local PE are connected to input ports. The main task of the input ports is to buffer incoming flits. To this end input ports include a FIFO buffer that can store up to 16 8-bit flits. The Xilinx coregen tool is used to generate efficient FIFO cores for the FPGA implementation. Outgoing channels are directly connected to input ports of neighboring routers, the composition of communication channels is depicted by Figure 6.1. The *full* signals indicates to a corresponding output port, whether the input buffer has free capacities. In this case, the output port can send a data flit on the *Data_out* bus to the *Data_in* bus of the corresponding input port. A *valid* signal indicates incoming data and is used at the input buffer as a write enable signal for the port's FIFO. The receiving of a flit is notified to the corresponding port by setting the *write* signal. If a new packet enters the input buffer, the port analyzes the header flit and requests the local crossbar by activating the *req* signal at the arbiter module.

Arbitration: A fixed priority grant-hold arbiter is used for switch arbitration. Figure 6.2 shows a schematic of the arbiter. Each of the five input ports is connected to the arbiter circuit through the signals *req*, *grant* and *release* signal. By setting the *req* signal, an input port can request access to

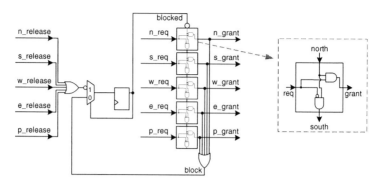

Figure 6.2: Schematic of the fixed priority arbiter.

the routers internal switch. If multiple ports request the switch at the same time the arbiter uses a fixed priority order of the ports, where the N port has the highest priority and the P port the lowest priority. Fixed priority arbiters are not fair, i.e., if a high priority port gets a grant and constantly demands the switch, any request from a lower priority port will not be served. However, the execution model rules out such a constant request of a single port, because the parallel applications typically synchronize at certain barriers and thus, all packets have to be received before more messages could be injected in succeeding algorithm phases. The grant-hold arbiter preserves the grant for a sending port until the message is forwarded completely. This is indicated by the incoming port with the *release* signal.

Flow control: Each buffer is connected with the corresponding neighboring router's arbiter through handshake signals. The NoC does not use virtual channels because XY-routing is inherently deadlock free and buffers are a very limited resource on the FPGA prototype. The wormhole routing strategy moves a data packet in form of a continuous stream of flits from the source node to the sink node. The first flit of a packet contains the target information used for routing computation, the final flit, called the tail flit, is marked with an control flag. When a port has gained access to the router's switch, it releases the grant after forwarding the tail flit of a package and all ports can subsequently arbitrate for the switch. Since it is assured, that the complete packet is available at the network interface before starting the transmission, flits pass the routers in a continuous manner.

6.2 Resource Utilization

Table 6.1 shows the resource utilization for many-core designs which use a hybrid interconnect including both, packet-switched routers and reconfigurable mesh SEs. Again, all measurements stem from an implementation on a Virtex-5 LX110T speedgrade-3 FPGA. A 4×4 system as shown in Figure 3.3(b), consumes merely one half of the device's logic resources and 27% of the slice registers. The largest prototype that can be successfully placed and routed on this FPGA is a 6×5 system which stresses the LUT resources up to 95%. As the device provides 64 DSP48E blocks and a Microblaze processor consumes 3 of such blocks for a build-in hardware multiplier, up to 21 cores can be equipped with a dedicated multiplier. For this reason, only the cores of the upper 4 rows of the 6×5 system support hardware multiplications.

An 8-bit RMESH SE consumes 133 LUTs which is merely 35% of the logic utilization of a 8-bit NoC router counterpart. To buffer the 8-bit data buses (plus a single valid bit) at the outgoing ports 36 flip-flops are utilized per SE. The router implements packet buffers in LUT shift registers, but still requires 286 slice registers. When taking into account both LUTs and registers and neglecting routing resources, one has to notice that the total area requirements of the 32-bit reconfigurable mesh network and the 8-bit NoC are roughly comparable. Since the reconfigurable mesh network is preferred for latency-critical operator multicast and the NoC for more flexible messaging, I have decided for a resource-balanced combination of an 8-bit NoC and a 32-bit reconfigurable mesh for the composition of the hybrid interconnect. In contrast to the data networks, the barrier core consumes a very limited amount of hardware resources as it requires only a simple interface to the FSL port.

6.3 Performance Evaluation

In this section I summarize experimental results measured on the presented architecture prototype. First, the broadcast and multicast performance of the proposed networks is quantified. Then, in the main part of this section I present Jacobi method algorithms compiled to the processor array and related runtime results when implementing communication by means of i) the reconfigurable mesh, ii) the NoC and iii) a combination of both, mesh and NoC networks.

Module	LUT	FF	DSP	BRAM	f_{max}
4×4 system	34612	18944	48	64	103MHz
	50%	27%	75%	43%	
6×5 system	66175	35352	60[1]	120	102MHz
	95%	51%	93%	81%	
NoC Router (8-bit)	385	286	0	0	247MHz[2]
NoC Router (32-bit)	679	398	0	0	240MHz[2]
RMESH SE (8-bit)	133	36	0	0	448MHz[2]
RMESH SE (32-bit)	446	132	0	0	448MHz[2]
Barrier core	6	3	0	0	519MHz[2]

[1]Nodes on row 1-4 with HW multiplier. [2]Synthesis estimations.

Table 6.1: Virtex-5 LX110T resource utilization for the many-core proto-types and the router/switch modules.

6.3.1 Operand Communication

To analyze the performance of the proposed networks, the runtimes for a single operand communication are measured on a 6×5 many-core prototype implementation running at 100MHz. The results are summarized in Table 6.2. When using the reconfigurable mesh based network, a single word broadcast (1:N communication pattern) from node 0 costs 74 cycles. In strong contrast, the NoC has to send 29 single messages to emulate the broadcast and that consumes 1118 cycles which is roughly 15x compared to the reconfigurable mesh based broadcast. For a single word message from node 0 to node 29 (1:1 communication pattern), the delay of the NoC is only 108 cycles or 1.5x of the reconfigurable mesh delay. The lower broadcast performance of the NoC is mainly due to overhead induced by creation and transportation of the header and the doubled per-hop latency of routers, compared to a SE.

A row multicast (1:k communication pattern) through the reconfigurable mesh network initiated by the nodes in the first column of the 6×5 prototype consumes 69 cycles. In contrast, sending 4 separate messages through the NoC consumes 297 cycles which is roughly 4.3x compared to the mesh based multicast.

As expected, the reconfigurable mesh network outperforms the NoC for single operand broadcasts and multicasts. The NoC can play out its strength when the communication pattern is more dynamic or if multiple nodes address a single reader (N:1 communication pattern). I have analyzed the latter

Pattern	Source	Sink	Network	T[cycles]
1:N	Node 0	Nodes 1–29	R-Mesh	74
			NoC	1118
1:1	Node 0	Node 29	R-Mesh	74
			NoC	108
1:k	Node 0	Nodes 1–4	R-Mesh	69
			NoC	297
N:1	Nodes 1–29	Node 0	R-Mesh	733
			NoC	402

Table 6.2: Runtime results for several operand communication patterns through reconfigurable mesh (R-Mesh) and NoC.

case through an example where all 29 nodes send to node 0 on the 30-node Microblaze prototype. When using the NoC, communication takes 402 cycles, whereas the reconfigurable mesh network consumes 733 cycles for the same operation. While the detailed comparison strongly depends on the underlying application and its communication requirements, the general rule is that with growing message sizes and more dynamic workloads, the NoC tends to outmatch the reconfigurable mesh network.

6.3.2 Case Study

The Jacobi method is an important algorithmic kernel used for solving linear equations of the form $Ax = b$. Based on an initial guess, the algorithm iteratively approximates the result vector x until it converges. I study the Jacoby method for matrix sizes that match the size of the processor array. Albeit this restricts the problem size to rather small matrices, one can more clearly compare the different communication alternatives. Using contraction mapping (c.f. Section 2.2.5), the problem size could be easily scaled by mapping larger computational portions to a single node. However, the contraction mapping approach makes the algorithms more complex and also suffers from limited scratchpad memory available at the processing cores while bringing only limited benefit for the analysis of the different communication styles. The implementations of the Jacobi method are tailored to the proposed on-chip interconnects and are outlined in Algorithm 6.1 and Algorithm 6.2.

Both algorithms start with a $p \times p$ matrix A distributed over an array of the same size. Processors located on the diagonal also store a corresponding entry of the result vector b. In any phase, both algorithms differentiate between processors which are responsible for the diagonal values of the matrix (*diagonal nodes*) and all other processors. Diagonal nodes first initialize their x_i, d, and v variables, all other nodes just the v variables. The actual iterative kernel is executed in a while loop until a convergence criterion is fulfilled. The kernel comprises two phases, each of which includes communication among cores. First, the actual solution vector is scattered over the columns of the array so that every non-diagonal node can compute $r = v \cdot x_i$ locally. Second, the new approximation of the vector x is computed solving the equation $x = \frac{1}{d}\left(r_i - \sum_{0 \le k < p, k \ne i} r_k\right)$ on every diagonal node.

Algorithm 6.1 shows how communication is implemented for the NoC. In the first phase (lines 7–16), the nodes on the diagonal address every other node in the same column i of the processor array to distribute their x_i values. In the second phase (lines 17–24), the nodes on the same row of the array send their multiplication results r to the diagonal nodes.

In Algorithm 6.2 both communication steps are handled via the reconfigurable mesh based network. At the beginning of the first phase (lines 7–15), the mesh is reconfigured to install column buses and the diagonal nodes broadcast their x_i variables. For the second phase (lines 16–33), the array gets synchronized and installs row buses. Since each of the $p - 1$ nodes has to send its partial result x_i to the diagonal node, this communication step comprises $p - 1$ separate broadcasts.

Algorithm 6.1: Parallel Jacobi method using the NoC interconnect.

Data: Matrices $A \in \mathbb{R}^{p,p}$ and $b \in \mathbb{R}^p$
Result: $x \in \mathbb{R}^p$, with $Ax = b$

```
 1  if Diagonal nodes P(i,i)
 2  │   xi ← a(i,i)   d ← a(i,i)   v
    │   ← bi
 3  else
 4  │   v ← a(i,j)
 5  endif
 6  while Convergence not reached do
 7  │   if Diagonal nodes P(i,i)
 8  │      for k ← 0 to p − 1 do
 9  │         if k ≠ i then
10  │         │   send(Pk,i, xi)
11  │         end
12  │      end
13  │      r ← v elsif Nodes P(i,j)
14  │      │   xi ← receive()
15  │      │   r ← v · xi
16  │   endif
17  │   if Diagonal nodes P(i,i)
18  │      for k ← 1 to p − 1 do
19  │      │   r ← r − receive()
20  │      end
21  │      r ← r/d   xi ← r
22  │   elsif Nodes P(i,j)
23  │      │   send(P(i,i), r)
24  │   endif
25  end
```

Algorithm 6.2: Parallel Jacobi method using the reconfigurable mesh interconnect.

Data: Matrices $A \in \mathbb{R}^{p,p}$ and $b \in \mathbb{R}^p$
Result: $x \in \mathbb{R}^p$, with $Ax = b$

```
 1  if Diagonal nodes P(i,i)
 2  │   xi ← a(i,i)   d ← a(i,i)   v
    │   ← bi
 3  else
 4  │   v ← a(i,j)
 5  endif
 6  while Convergence not reached do
 7  │   sync
 8  │   swconf(NS)
 9  │   if Diagonal nodes P(i,i)
10  │      broadcast(xi)
11  │      r ← v
12  │   elsif Nodes P(i,j)
13  │      │   xi ← read()
14  │      │   r ← v · xi
15  │   endif
16  │   sync
17  │   swconf(WE)
18  │   if Diagonal nodes P(i,i)
19  │      for k ← 1 to p − 1 do
20  │      │   r ← r − read()
21  │      end
22  │      r ← r/d   xi ← r
23  │   elsif Nodes P(i,j)
24  │      for k ← 0 to p − 1 do
25  │      │   if k ≠ i then
26  │      │      if j = k
27  │      │      │   broadcast(xi)
28  │      │      else
29  │      │      │   read()
30  │      │      endif
31  │      │   end
32  │      end
33  │   endif
34  end
```

6.3.3 Runtime Results

Table 6.3 summarizes the runtime measurements for the different Jacobi algorithms on FPGA many-core prototypes. I have studied arrays of size 5×5 and 4×4. As mentioned in Section 3.4.2, the used target device features only 21 hardware multipliers. Thus, the cores of the 5×5 array use software mul-

	Size	Interconnect	T[cycles]	$I(abs)$
HW mul.	1		380318	1
	4×4	NoC	58772	6.47
	4×4	Reconfigurable mesh	66797	5.69
	4×4	Combined	57255	6.64
SW mul.	1		477014	
	4×4	NoC	70859	6.73
	4×4	Reconfigurable mesh	87079	5.48
	4×4	Combined	67579	7.06
SW mul.	1		749060	
	5×5	NoC	77580	9.66
	5×5	Reconfigurable mesh	110076	6.80
	5×5	Combined	72359	10.35

Table 6.3: Runtime comparison for $k = 30$ iterations of the Jacobi method algorithms.

tiplication, whereas the smaller sized prototype can also perform hardware multiplication. The first column of Table 6.3 indicates the multiplier implementation, and the second column specifies the array size. Column three lists the used interconnect and column four presents the runtime in clock cycles. Results for array size 1 are acquired from a sequential Jacobi algorithm executed on a single Microblaze node. The right-most column of Table 6.3 displays the absolute runtime improvement factor over the single core implementation, $I(abs)$. After $k = 30$ iteration steps, the derivation between the exact solution and the approximated result was measured to be around 1% in all of the presented test cases. Hence, all the experiments are based on this number of iterations.

The absolute improvements for the parallelized Jacobi algorithms for the different communication styles and array dimensions are graphically depicted in Figure 6.3. On both the 4×4 and the 5×5 platform, the pure NoC implementation excels over the reconfigurable mesh based network. However, the Jacobi algorithm case study does not fully exploit the performance of reconfigurable mesh based multicasts. The NoC can emulate a row/column multicast with just 3 or 4 separate messages, respectively. With regard to the results presented in Section 6.3.1, I expect higher performance gains for the reconfigurable mesh when scaling the array size.

The prototypes that execute multiplications in software deliver higher im-

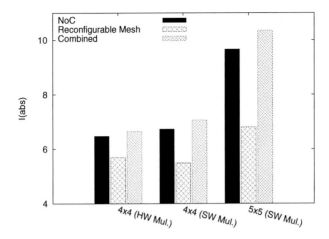

Figure 6.3: Absolute runtime improvement factors for the parallel Jacobi method on different array sizes and different communication styles.

provement factors. This is due to the fact that the parallelizable portion of the program grows because the multiplications inside the kernel take more time.

As a third alternative, a combined algorithm is studied that employs the reconfigurable mesh based network for broadcasts on columns (lines 7–15 of Algorithm 6.2) and the NoC for transmitting values from the row cores to the diagonal nodes (lines 17–24 of Algorithm 6.1). Interleaving both networks in this cooperative manner leads to better results in any case, with more emphasized gains for the larger sized array.

6.4 Chapter Conclusion

This chapter introduced a hybrid interconnect for a many-core comprising reconfigurable mesh, NoC and barrier networks. I present details of the implementation and give results for both, single operand broadcast/multicast operations and a Jacobi algorithm case study. While generally the reconfigurable mesh excels for single operand broadcasts and multicasts, the NoC is advantageous for larger message sizes and dynamic workloads. However, the main result of the experiments is that a proper combination of both the reconfigurable mesh and the NoC achieves the highest runtime improvements. When designing parallel algorithms the programmer usually has detailed knowledge about the required communication patterns. In particular, this holds true for regular, data-parallel algorithms, e.g., operations on multidimensional arrays, where multicast communication often follows certain structures such as sending data to adjacent processors in the same row, column or block of the array. By exploiting this knowledge in form of proper reconfigurable mesh based messaging, the programmer can significantly reduce communication costs.

CHAPTER 7

Program Driven Power Management

This chapter tackles the issue of saving power when executing parallel applications on the presented many-core architecture prototypes. Power consumption has been identified as a primary design constraint [118] and the erstwhile maxim that "chip area is expensive and power is for free" has turned into its opposite. Of course, area will always be limited, but the increase of chip area Moore's law offers can only be utilized if a certain power budget is satisfied.

For a rigorous reduction of energy consumption optimization techniques have to be applied on all levels of the design process. High optimizations can be achieved at the technology layer were new materials and processes can lead to significant power savings. First of all, miniaturization of devices is accompanied with a shrinking supply voltage and results in lower leakage and dynamic power consumption per transistor. Other achievements are due to better transistor technology, for example, the replacement of silicon dioxide gate dielectrics with new hafnium-based high-k dielectric. On the logic level, techniques like clock gating and asynchronous logic are used to reduce energy. Regarding the microarchitectural design of processor cores, optimizations like circuit-level timing speculation [53] are used. At run-time, dynamic frequency/voltage scaling is a powerful method to reduce the processors energy consumption during phases of low utilization.

In this work, I focus on power optimizations on the higher design levels. An evident characteristic of reconfigurable mesh algorithms is, that a substantial proportion of the PEs might not by used during certain algorithm steps.

Furthermore, PEs which are used for computation are frequently idle, because they have to wait for remote data to arrive. This observations can be also carried over to other massively parallel architectures.

As the cores of the many-core prototypes do not operate in a multi-threading mode, they are either *active, waiting* (for data) or *unused*. This peculiarity can be leveraged for power management, by properly switching unused PEs to an energy-efficient state. An ideal method for lowering dynamic power consumption at a minimal latency is clock gating. On FPGA technology, one can differentiate between two variants of clock gating: a dedicated signal, i.e., a stall signal, can be used to control i) the clock enable inputs of the flip-flops or ii) the built-in clock network itself. The second approach is more power efficient than the first one, with improvements of about 13.5% on average as stated in [172]. However, controlling the clock network is also less flexible due to the limited number of internal clock buffers. For example, Virtex-4 devices come with 32 global clock lines, each of which can be driven by one clock buffer. Due to this limitation this method can not be used for the reconfigurable mesh prototypes presented in this thesis as usually many more than 32 individual processors have to be controlled independently.

I propose two strategies for reducing energy consumption. First, if a core is known to be "unused" for a certain amount of algorithm steps, it is caused to switch to a low-power mode until it is used again in the algorithm. I call this strategy *sleep-while-unused*. Second, if a writing node is known to access a sub-bus, which requires some waiting time until the communication step completes, I force only the writing node to actively wait for the completion and keep all other nodes on the sub-bus in the low-power mode. Upon completion of the communication step, all nodes on the sub-bus are notified to continue. This *sleep-while-waiting* approach is particularly relevant for the Picoblaze reconfigurable mesh prototype, because its need to abide a certain waiting time for any communication step of an algorithm.

7.1 Power Management for Microblaze PEs

The Microblaze core does not incorporate a low-power mode as many other microcontroller cores do. However, if the Microblaze pipeline is stalled, the dynamic power dissipation is considerably reduced and thus, halting the pipeline can be used as low-power mode. One method to force the Microblaze core to stall its pipeline is to exploit the build-in capabilities of the FSL communication links. When a Microblaze core has finished the current superstep's computation phase or if it is not even used in the current superstep it executes a `sync` instruction to wait until all nodes have finished the superstep. Technically, the `sync` results in a blocking FSL *get* operation that runs to completion when the last node reaches its barrier synchronization statement of the current superstep. Being blocked, the Microblaze pipeline is stalled and the dynamic power dissipation is reduced to a minimum.

The *sleep-while-unused* and *sleep-while-waiting* principles are automatically handled by using the blocking FSL instructions. If not used, the Microblaze calls a barrier synchronization and goes to sleep (stall) mode. When a core waits for incoming data, i.e., it has executed a blocking `fslget` instruction on the data port, it gets stalled as long as the data is not available.

7.2 Power Management Model for ARMLang

For the use of fine-grained power management in ARMLang the language was extended by two keywords SLEEP and WAKEUP. If a node executes a SLEEP instruction, the PE is immediately stalled, while the SE and the local network interface remain active. If one (or multiple) of the remaining active nodes execute a *WAKEUP*, all nodes of the processor array are notified to continue.

The Picoblaze core natively does not come with any stalling capabilities. Therefore, I have modified the Picoblaze design to support a stall mode in which switching activity inside the processor is significantly reduced. In particular, the Picoblaze design is extended by an incoming stall signal which is used to disable the program counter and to prevent the registers from being written[1]. The energy savings, caused by the stall mechanism have to be judged against the energy overhead caused by the controller which manages stalling. As a very simplistic controller is used, this overhead is negligible.

Using ARMLang, the programmer is able to instruct a group of cores to immediately switch to the low-power mode. A wakeup brings the cores back to the normal mode. Let T^m be the runtime of a reconfigurable mesh algorithm which is augmented with power management instructions and T_i^+ the portion of time processor i spends in full-power mode. As reconfigurable mesh algorithms often show a very deterministic behavior, T^m and T_i^+ can be determined statically. The dynamic power dissipation P^m for ARMLang

---

[1] In 10/2010 a version of the Picoblaze that is optimized to the 6-LUT architecture of Xilinx Virtex-6/Spartan-6 devices was released (called *kcpsm6*). This version introduces a new *sleep* input signal that implements the same functionality as the *stall* signal described here.

algorithms which utilize power management can be estimated as follows:

$$P^m = \sum_{i=0}^{N-1} \left(\frac{T_i^+}{T^m} P^+ + \left(1 - \frac{T_i^+}{T^m} \right) P^- \right) \tag{7.1}$$

Here, P^+ is the average power a reconfigurable mesh tile dissipates in the general mode and P^- the average power dissipated in low-power mode. As each processor might spend a different portion of time in the low-power mode, the sum over all N tiles of the mesh has to be computed.

If power management is not used, the algorithm takes T^g time and the average power P^g is simply estimated as:

$$P^g = N \cdot P^+ \tag{7.2}$$

Knowing both, the improved and the general power dissipation, one can calculate the percentage of the power reduction as follows:

$$P' = \frac{P^g - P^m}{P^g} \cdot \frac{T^g}{T^m} \tag{7.3}$$

The factor T^g/T^m covers the slowdown that might occur when using power management instructions. This factor is usually small, as the power management instructions can normally be hidden behind the waiting time. An extensive evaluation of the power management model is given in Section 7.3.

7.3 Analysis of Power Management Techniques

7.3.1 Experimental Set-up

To measure the power consumption of the reconfigurable mesh architecture, I use the XUP Virtex-II Pro development board. The XUP board supports individual supplies for the core voltage of 1.5 V (V_{CCINT}) as well as for the 2.5 V/3.3 V general purpose voltages and I/O voltages (V_{CC2V5}/V_{CC3V3}). Each of the three on-board power supplies can be disabled and replaced by an external supply.

Figure 7.1 sketches the experimental setup. An ammeter is interposed into the V_{CCINT} core power rail in order to measure the energy dissipated by the implemented logic. An additional voltmeter is used to monitor and level the core voltage at the demanded 1.5 volt. The use of an ammeter only allows

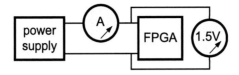

Figure 7.1: Experimental setup for practical power measurements.

for very coarse-grained measurements. Hence, I measure the average current for a specific application pattern which is executed inside an infinite loop.

The XUP board with its ability to access the internal power rail of the FPGA is a perfect vehicle for practical power measurements. However, since the device is relatively small, one can not directly measure power consumptions for larger reconfigurable mesh prototypes running more realistic workloads. Hence, typical patterns are executed to achieve useful approximations on how power management techniques will impact power dissipation of reconfigurable mesh algorithms on a 16 × 16 prototype implemented on a larger Virtex-4 device.

7.3.2 Power Consumption of Mesh Tiles

The three sources of power dissipation in CMOS technology are switching power, short circuit power and leakage power, where the latter states the static part and the first two state the dynamic part of the power dissipation. In the experiments, especially the dynamic power consumed by the design is of interest. As merely the overall current can be measured in the experimental setup, the static current has to be substracted. Static current can be estimated by measuring the current when the device is "doing nothing". Determining what "doing nothing" actually means for an FPGA is far from being trivial. The two common ways for estimating the static current are to measure the power consumption of either an unconfigured device or of a configured device which is not clocked. The experiments reveal as a lowest current 53 mA (79.5 mW) when measuring an unconfigured device. This nicely corresponds to the Xilinx Virtex-II Pro data sheet which quotes a typical quiescent V_{CCINT} supply current of 50 mA for the specific device [184]. When quantifying the current of a configured device, for which the clock input is tied to low, measurements show a current of 14 mA (21 mW) for a reconfigurable mesh array with 16 nodes. For the following calculations, the value of 21 mW is used as an estimate for the static power.

117

Communication pattern	16-core (measured) [mA]	16-core (dynamic) [mA]	4-core (measured) [mA]	4-core (dynamic) [mA]	Current per node [mA]	Power per node [mW]
Column broadcasts	450	397	180	127	22.5	33.75
Neighbor communication	457	404	182	129	22.92	34.38
Maximal load	480	427	193	140	23.92	35.88

Table 7.1: Power measurement results for three typical communication patterns.

For determining the power consumption of a single reconfigurable mesh tile, I implement several reconfigurable meshes of varying size and measure the average current for different programs. Table 7.1 summarizes some measurement results. For a 4×4 reconfigurable mesh prototype that executes an odd-even transposition sort algorithm, the total current is measured to be $457\,mA$. Subtracting the static current of $14\,mA$ results in a dynamic current of $443\,mA$. Compared to a 4×1 prototype, executing the same algorithm, the additional 12 cores cause an amount of $275\,mA$ of additional current. Hence, one tile approximately requires $22.92\,mA$ at $1.5\,V$, which results in a power dissipation of $34.38\,mW$. The host subsystem dissipates $114.42\,mW$. As odd-even transposition sort has a very typical behavior for algorithms that use neighbor communication, the result is representative for a broader class of algorithms. Table 7.1 shows two other classes for typical patterns. Column broadcasts depicts algorithms with longer communication phases and, due to the waiting times, a relatively small amount of computation steps. In contrast, the maximal load pattern characterizes algorithms with a high computation/communication ratio.

To measure average power for certain ARMLang instruction classes, I execute characteristic algorithms inside a loop while using the initial input data in every iteration. The measurements show that the execution of typical ALU operations consumes about $28.2\,mW$ per tile, while the execution of control-flow dominated patterns dissipates about $34.6\,mW$ power per tile. By comparing the power dissipation to algorithms where more and more cores are forced to the stall mode instead of executing NOPs, the power dissipation can be reduced by 40.5%. That is, instead of $34.38\,mW$ in the normal mode, a tile only consumes $20.45\,mW$ in the stall mode.

For measuring the power dissipation caused by the interconnection network, the switches are configured to install a circular bus structure and inject one or multiple messages onto the bus. All PEs are put into sleep mode and, thus, the messages cycle infinitely. If no message is inserted, the completely stalled array consumes $328\,mW$. When inserting one message the power dissipation increases to $376\,mW$, if every second processor injects a message, measurements show a power dissipation of $449.5\,mW$. While the first pattern matches the network load in case of a global broadcast, the second one models a high network load.

Apparently, the consumed power also depends on placement and routing of the many-core system. To that end, I have conducted experiments with differently placed and routed designs. The deviations in consumed power between these designs are limited by approximately 5% which justifies the neglection of placement and routing in the analysis.

7.3.3 Comparing Measurements and Estimations

The Xilinx ISE tools include XPower Analyzer (XPA) as a tool for power examination of Xilinx devices. Using capacity models for low-level hardware components (LUTs, RAMs, wires, etc.) XPA is able to analyze dynamic power dissipation for placed and routed designs. While XPA can calculate approximations for a static design, the generation of more reliable data needs detailed knowledge about the switching activity of all the logic and wires in the design. These data can be generated by timing simulation with, e.g., Modelsim. While such a fine-grained analysis tends to produce accurate energy estimates, the generation of simulation dumps and the estimation process itself are usually extremely time consuming and produce enormous amounts of data. On a 2.4 GHz Intel Core 2 Duo CPU with 8 GB RAM a $200\,\mu s$ simulation of a 4×4 reconfigurable mesh prototype system takes 33 minutes and produces 6.2 GB of simulation data. The power estimation process then takes additional 43 minutes.

Table 7.2 shows some XPA power estimations for a reconfigurable mesh addition algorithm (see Section 7.3.4) on the 4×4 prototype running at 100 MHz. When analyzed without any toggle rate information, XPA estimates a total power of $445\,mW$ for the design. The estimation for the whole program, including the generation of random data and serial output by the Microblaze

Estimation modality	Total Power
Static (no simulation data)	445 mW
Complete execution time	974 mW
R-Mesh bin-tree addition (incl. I/O)	840 mW
R-Mesh bin-tree addition (w/o I/O)	754 mW

Table 7.2: XPower estimations for the reconfigurable mesh bin-tree addition algorithm.

host, is $974\,mW$. For comparison to the presented experiments, the periods from the simulation dump in which the reconfigurable mesh coprocessor has been active were isolated. Power estimation runs for this case show $840\,mW$ when the transfer of data to and from the mesh is included, and $754\,mW$ when looking just at the algorithm kernel. Compared to the measurements of $676.5\,mW$, the deviation is about 10%.

7.3.4 Saving Power by Sleep-while-unused

This section provides an example for a typical reconfigurable mesh algorithm in which some nodes are only used for a certain portion of time. At first, estimates for the power consumption caused by executing the algorithm in both, the general mode and the power managed mode are presented. As the algorithm can be usefully implemented on a small size 4×4 prototype, the estimations are verified by measurements.

As an example algorithm, the binary tree simulation on the reconfigurable mesh is choosen. A binary tree with 2^h leaf nodes can be simulated by a reconfigurable mesh of size 2^h in h steps. As a core operation, any associative and commutative binary operator can be applied. In the following, the algorithm is used for adding up numbers.

On a 4×4 reconfigurable mesh the bin-tree algorithm for adding 2^4 values operates in 4 steps. The 16 numbers are stored, one value each, in the processors. In the first step of the algorithm, pairs of adjacent nodes get connected by bus reconfiguration. On each sub-bus, the node with higher identifier writes its value onto the bus, the node with lower identifier reads the bus and adds the received value to the locally stored number. For the rest of the algorithm, each node that has written its value does not have to execute any useful computation. Only the SEs have to remain active, as data has to be routed through the nodes. Thus, after each step, one half of the processors can be switched off, as the following algorithm steps work analogously. Note, that the distances between active processors are getting longer and longer. Hence, the later steps of the algorithm, where less processors are used take more runtime (spent for communication).

For a detailed analysis of the algorithm, I look at the assembly instructions which are executed on the single PEs. The algorithm takes 37 assembly instructions, 4 additional instructions are used to manage an infinite loop. Regarding all nodes, $41 \cdot 16 = 656$ instructions have to be executed, 287 of them in full-power or general mode. As the operations which are executed on the processors in full-power mode are very similar to the column broadcast pattern, one can estimate $P^+ = 33.75\ mW$ following Table 7.1. For the low-power mode P^- I use the measured value of $20.45\ mW$. Taking these numbers, one can calculate P^m according to Equation 7.1:

$$
\begin{aligned}
P^m &= \sum_{i=0}^{N-1} \left(\frac{T_i^+}{T^m} \right) P^+ + \sum_{i=0}^{N-1} \left(1 - \frac{T_i^+}{T^m} \right) P^- \\
&= 7 \cdot 33.75\ mW + 9 \cdot 20.45\ mW \\
&= 420.3\ mW
\end{aligned}
$$

Following Equation 7.2, the power for the algorithm executed in general mode is $P^g = 16 \cdot 33.75\ mW = 540\ mW$. Since the instructions for managing the low power mode can not be completely hidden behind the waiting time, the slowdown factor for the power reduced algorithm is $T^g/T^m = 39/41$. Following Equation 7.3, this results in an improvement

$$
P' = \frac{540 - 420.3}{540} \cdot \frac{39}{41} = 21.09\%.
$$

To verify the estimations, the actual power consumption of the addition algorithm was measured on the 4×4 reconfigurable mesh prototype. Without power management the algorithm consumes $676.5\ mW$. Subtracting $21\ mW$ static power and $114.42\ mW$ for the host system results in a dynamic power dissipation of $541.08\ mW$ caused by the reconfigurable mesh. This result is highly consistent (0.2% derivation) with the calculated estimation of P^g which was $540\ mW$. When enabling power management, the algorithm dissipates $570\ mW$. Subtracting static power and power dissipation caused by the host results in an remaining amount of $434.58\ mW$. This measurement is $14.28\ mW$ or 3.4% higher than the calculated value for P^m. I designate this value to be the overhead for the slightly increased logic activity caused by the wake-up mechanism. All results are summarized in Table 7.3.

	P^g	P^m
Power Model [mW]	540	420.3
Power Measurements [mW]	541.08	434.58
Derivation	0.2%	3.6%

Table 7.3: Power results for the addition algorithm.

7.3.5 Saving Power by Sleep-while-waiting

A second method for reducing dynamic power consumption is to stall reader nodes during communication phases. Listing 7.1 shows two different methods to implement a row broadcast in ARMLang. In both cases the left-most processors of the rows broadcast their a value on the bus. When data has reached all reader nodes, the nodes' processors read the data into their b variable. In Listing 7.1(a) every processor actively executes no-operation instructions. For all but the nodes of the first column waiting time is specified through the WAIT statement. The first column nodes also execute no-operations, which is caused by path equalization automatically done by the ARMLang compiler when translating the WHERE-ELSEWHERE statement. The same operation is implemented slightly different in Listing 7.1(b). In this example, only the the first column nodes call a WAIT statement, while every other node switches into the sleep mode. The time between the initial WRITE and the READ instruction is exactly the same.

Measuring the power dissipation for both examples reveals that the first method consumes $568mW$ and the second one between $331mW$ and $428.5mW$ depending on the length of the bus and thus, the waiting time. This again results in a reduction in power dissipation (and energy, as the operations take exactly the same amount of time) ranging from 26.2% to 44.4% for a node that is stalled instead of executing active waiting.

The benefit of the sleep-while-waiting method increases with the waiting times inherent in the algorithm. In Section 5.1.1 a sparse matrix multiplication on a 16×16 Picoblaze-based reconfigurable mesh is presented. In this algorithm, the waiting times depend on the sparseness factor. Figure 7.2 shows the comparison of the estimated energy consumption between the original and the power-managed implementation. For this example, the overall energy dissipation can be reduced by 16.39% in average with respect to the sparseness factor. The energy savings for this application are naturally be-

```
WHERE PID%WIDTH == 0          WHERE PID%WIDTH == 0
  SWITCH E;                     SWITCH E;
  WRITE(a)                      WRITE(a)
ELSEWHERE                       WAIT(WIDTH);
  SWITCH WE;                  ELSEWHERE
  WAIT(WIDTH)                   SWITCH WE;
END;                            SLEEP
READ(b);                      END;
                              WAKEUP;
                              READ(b);
```

(a)   (b)

Listing 7.1: Two alternative implementations of a row broadcast in
ARMLang: Active waiting (a) and the sleep-while-waiting
approach (b).

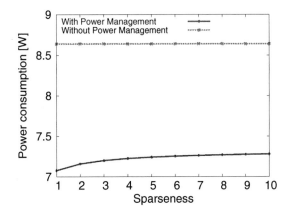

Figure 7.2: Estimations for power dissipation of a 16×16 reconfigurable mesh
sparse matrix multiplication algorithm.

low the reported maximum power savings of up to 44% because the approach
reduces power dissipation only during communication phases.

7.4 Chapter Conclusion

In this chapter, I have introduced power management techniques for reconfigurable mesh many-cores. Since the reconfigurable mesh has mainly been
a theoretical vehicle, power and energy have not yet been considered for this
massively parallel architecture. In particular, I propose and investigate two
methods for reducing power dissipation in reconfigurable mesh algorithms.
The sleep-while-unused method takes advantage of an inherent characteristic
of many reconfigurable mesh algorithms that allows to shut down a number of nodes while the algorithm progresses. The sleep-while-waiting method
forces nodes that wait for the completion of a communication step into a sleep
mode. Sleep-while-waiting reduces the dynamic energy consumption during
communication phases by up to 44%. To support the program-driven power
management techniques, the architecture is augmented by a control network
and the programming language ARMLang is extended by two additional keywords. By means of example algorithms, I demonstrate the efficiency of the
two methods and achieve a reduction in power consumption of 21.09% and
16.39%, respectively.

CHAPTER 8

Conclusions and Future Research

This chapter summarizes the thesis and draws a conclusion based on the presented results. Additionally, further areas of research are presented that exploit the potential of reconfigurable mesh based many-cores.

8.1 Summary

This thesis presents an approach to reduce the reconfigurable mesh model to practice. There is a notable discrepancy between the extent of theoretical results and the practical impact of reconfigurable meshes. At the time when researchers came up with the model, the design of parallel computers evolved in a completely different direction. The technology circumstances spurred the microprocessor boom and repressed emerging massively parallel processing platforms. But new design constraints, primarily energy budgeting, will certainly lead to a continued evolution of increased on-chip parallelism. The reconfigurable mesh model is one potential candidate to exploit the massive amount of parallelism on future processors.

Designing a reconfigurable mesh computer that profits from the model in practice leads to several challenges. To address these challenges, I contribute a practical review of the reconfigurable mesh programming model for many-cores.In particular, this thesis comprises the following main contributions:

- I present a framework for generating, programming and debugging reconfigurable mesh architectures based on two industry standard soft processor cores of varying granularity and self-developed switch elements. The many-cores are designed to support the single-program multiple-data (SPMD) way of programming. Beside pure reconfigurable mesh algorithms, also stencil codes or systolic algorithms can be efficiently implemented that way. Using the established prototype implementations, I provide the first ever practical study of word-level reconfigurable meshes implemented in FPGA technology.

- In this thesis, I introduce the new programming language ARMLang and present the implementation of a corresponding compiler. ARMLang specifications are discrete programs that can be compiled to regular arrays of processors which are connected through a reconfigurable mesh interconnect. A distinctive feature of ARMLang is path balancing for time-deterministic processors like the Picoblaze.

- A packet-switched NoC architecture is developed and integrated to the many-core as an extension to the reconfigurable mesh communication capabilities. The light-weight NoC implementation is optimized for point-to-point signaling of operands. The network interfaces are directly connected to the processor core which allows a very low latency access to the core's registers. Results show that the data networks outperform each other for different communication requirements so that a combined use increases the system's performance.

- A further extension of the on-chip networks is an ultra-low overhead global barrier network. The network is able to evaluate a global synchronization in the order of few clock cycles.

- I exploit the typical deterministic behavior of reconfigurable meshes to minimize the energy consumption. To this end, I introduce the two techniques called *sleep-while-unused* and *sleep-while-waiting*. I evaluate both techniques by means of case studies and measure energy reductions of 21% and 16%, respectively. In order to apply the proposed energy optimization techniques, the initial algorithms do not have to be modified at all or only to some small extet.

8.2 Conclusions

This thesis provides essential insights into the question of whether the reconfigurable mesh is an adequate architecture and programming model for many-core processors. My work fundamentally rests on FPGA implementations which evidently shows that reconfigurable mesh processors with hundreds of autonomous cores are feasible to be built. The effectiveness of programming for the massively parallel processors is demonstrated by several case studies for various prototypes. Based on the presented results and my experiences, I illustrate why the reconfigurable mesh is not only a possible but also a suitable model for many-cores. To this end, I point out four aspects which are of specific interest and which are tackled in this thesis:

Signal propagation delay When analyzing the reconfigurable mesh model under practical considerations, the most evident discrepancy is the required constant time broadcast delay. No current technology can, theoretically, implement such feature as no information can be transmitted faster than the speed of light. *In practice, signals that stay on-chip can be transmitted very fast.* For the presented reconfigurable mesh network data moves through the network one hop per cycle. So, for a reconfigurable mesh processor arrays with reasonable size the latency of a broadcast step is in the order of some clock cycles.

Additionally, the presented router and the several SE of the reconfigurable mesh can be clocked faster than the PEs. I have implemented an array of 4×4 Microblaze cores connected through a hybrid network much like the depicted prototypes in Chapter 6 but attached each building block – PE, SE and router – to its own clock domain. The Microblaze PEs were operating at 100 MHz, the routers at 200 MHz and the SEs at 250 MHz. This enhancement does not afford much modification, as the network interfaces are FIFO based and the applied FIFO cores can be configured to operate asynchronously. This way, the actual transportation of data can be sped up by 2x and 2.5x, respectively.

For the majority of word-level reconfigurable mesh algorithms, a broadcast delay of several cycles is fairly acceptable. Bit-level algorithms typically have very different characteristics. They do not exchange data in the classical sense, but use communication for computation. For example, the XOR algorithm reconfigures the SEs, broadcasts a signal from a specific node and, to compute the result, detects the sink of the signal at the boundary PEs. Due to their characteristics, bit-level algorithms are very dependent on the broadcast delay and are not suited for the proposed many-core architecture.

In contrast to the reconfigurable mesh network which is optimized for latency, the presented NoC architecture is more beneficial in terms of throughput and flexibility. Each node can address any other node directly. This information, given in the header of a data packet, leads to certain overheads. The header has to be processed by each router on the path which causes additional energy consumption and increases the latency of the transmission. Although the network interface to the NoC is kept very lightweight, the generation and also the receiving of a message consumes a reasonable amount of time.

As a result, I propose a hybrid network architecture for many-cores that are designed to execute general SPMD programs. The low latency reconfigurable mesh network is well suited for communicating operands among groups of nodes that can connect to the same bus segment. If message sizes grow or the structure of communication gets more irregular, the packet-switched NoC is beneficial.

Algorithmic scalability The second main practical shortcoming of the reconfigurable mesh is the dependency of the mesh size on the input size. For a serial programming model, the underlying architecture is fixed and an algorithm's runtime can be expressed as a function of the input size. For reconfigurable meshes, it is just the other way around; the execution time is fixed (or a very slow growing function) and the number of required PEs grows with the input. *I would characterize this issue as the main challenge for a practical realization of the reconfigurable mesh model.*

Although algorithmic scalability is not the main concern of this thesis, I provide several results to this problem. In contrast to general reconfigurable mesh models that support a large variety of switch patterns, restricted models support efficient self-simulation. The presented implementation of the HV-RN self-simulation strategy applied to an add-reduce algorithm shows that the overhead of general scaling simulations is substantially high. In contrast, scaling the algorithm itself causes an improved runtime compared to the original algorithm running on a sufficiently large mesh. In other words, a specially scaled algorithm can speed up the computation although running on a fraction of PEs.

Reconfigurable mesh programming One important question is, whether developing reconfigurable mesh programs is viable for general software programmers. On the one hand, several reconfigurable mesh algorithms are very sophisticated, but this holds also true for many optimized sequential algorithms. On the other hand, many problems are already solved for the reconfigurable mesh model. The missing link between reconfigurable mesh algorithms and a reconfigurable mesh processor is a proper programming language and compiler. *In this thesis I show* *that reconfigurable mesh programs can be specified relatively easy.* The programming flow for processor cores that already supports a high-level language can be extended so that compile-time information is exploited by a preprocessor to generate core-specific code. For more lightweight PEs like microcontrollers or programmable state machines, I propose a tool flow that generates target code out of a newly defined language ARMLang. The ARMLang compiler is specified on a very abstract level. This approach is beneficial for multiple reasons. First, it allows to easily port the backend to processors with an instruction set architecture similar to the Picoblaze. Second, new language constructs can be integrated rapidly.

The global synchrony can be induced by structuring the program into super-steps which are ensured through a fast barrier network. For the presented many-cores with up to 256 Picoblaze cores or 36 Microblaze cores, the combinational barrier network could be evaluated in a single CPU cycle. For larger arrays, the signal propagation should be extended by pipeline registers. But in any case, the evaluation of simple AND or OR reductions can be done very fast. An example is the Blue Gene\L System that implements a similar barrier network with a round-trip latency of less than 1.5 μs for a system size of 65,536 nodes [66]. The implementation of the barrier network and the required network interfaces to the PEs presented in this thesis lead to a very limited resource overhead. If PEs are used that allow for a deterministic analysis of execution time, a compiler can generate target code that balances the program paths of all cores to keep the execution in lock-step.

Energy efficiency Providing comparative results for the energy efficiency of a prototype system is an ambiguous problem. Power characteristics heavily depend on the present technology of the processor. Especially, comparing FPGA-based designs with custom ASICs is typically misleading. For this reason, I put the focus on how to reduce energy consumption for the proposed architecture and measured energy reductions of more than 20% on running prototypes.

A question that remains open is how energy efficient reconfigurable mesh processor arrays are compared to other parallel architectures. *The assumption is that the inherent determinism and the massive parallelism of reconfigurable mesh algorithms will certainly have a positive impact on the energy consumption.* To use simple but many processing cores per die is a principle to lower a chip's energy per se. How the system can profit from the information of which cores are not busy with actual computation is shown in Chapter 7. A further question is how energy efficient the scheduled communication style of the reconfigurable mesh is in itself. I estimate that the energy consumption decreases compared to packet-switched networks, because no packet processing and packet buffering is required.

8.3 Outlook

The goal of this thesis is to provide a practical approach to the reconfigurable mesh model. There remains a multitude of open problems but also opportunities for future research. From my point of view, two directions are of particular interest, the investigation of *advanced scaling simulation techniques* and analyzing the applicability of the reconfigurable mesh model for *emerging interconnect technologies*.

Although a multitude of scaling simulations has been developed, it is still not sufficiently evaluated how efficient these scaling techniques are in practice. My experiments show that a custom scaling outclasses even an optimal self-simulation technique. It would be very beneficial to establish a general approach to combine serial algorithms and reconfigurable mesh algorithms in order to make codes scalable on reconfigurable mesh hardware.

Recently, the reconfigurable mesh model was applied in the context of emerging communication technologies, among which are optical interconnects [54] [187] and spin-waves [55] [57] [58]. Other recent proposals investigate nanophotonic interconnects, e.g., a photonic crossbar architecture [162] or a hybrid photonic/electric NoC [145]. All these technologies have very different characteristics compared to classical electrical interconnects. Unlike traditional electric signaling, communicating via light- or spin-waves does not need the transportation of an electric charge. The process of charging and discharging conventional communication circuits consumes substantial energy, in particular for global or inter-core wires and for that reason it seems very promising to replace traditional global communication architectures. The benefits of such technology are encouraging; huge bandwidth, very low latency, and exceedingly low energy dissipation. However, one could hardly implement conventional NoCs on the basis of light-waves or spin-waves because these technologies lack necessary functions for packet switching: buffering and processing. The reconfigurable mesh model, in turn, does not require packet buffers nor processing of data at each hop on the communication path; the switches only need to set the direction of signal flow once per communication phase. This feature nicely fits to the properties of light-waves as well as spin-waves because they can both be switched by electronically controlled switches.

Finally, I believe that the methods and tools presented in this thesis provide an appropriate environment to further study reconfigurable mesh algorithms in practice. The hardware architecture can be adopted since the platform is implemented in FPGA technology. Interfaces between PEs and SEs/routers are kept clear to facilitate the rapid integration of new processor cores. Also the programming environment is designed to allow for extensive modifications. The presented NoC architecture is applicable for general FPGA many-cores, no matter whether an SPMD style of programming is used or not. In conclusion, the presented framework and methods represent essential tools for further research.

APPENDIX A

Selective Source Files

A.1 Context-free grammar for ARMLang

Listing A.1 shows the context-free grammar of ARMLang in Extended BackusNaur Form (EBNF). The specification can be straightforwardly transformed to a GENTLE parser. For each production rule of the EBNF a corresponding *nonterm* rule has to be created. Each alternative for one production rule, is translated to a *rule* statement in GENTLE.

```
Program ::= "PROGRAM" Ident "(" Number ":" Number ")" ";"

DeclList ::= Decl ";" DeclList | Decl

Decl ::= Ident ":" Type

Type ::= Scalar | Vector

Scalar ::= "INTEGER"

Vector ::= "ARRAY" "[" PIDExpression ".." PIDExpression "]" "OF" Scalar

StatSeq ::= Stat | StatSeq ";" Stat

Stat ::= "SYNC" | "SLEEP" | "WAKEUP"
    | "WHERE" PIDRelationList "DO" StatSeq "END"
    | "WHERE" PIDRelationList "DO" StatSeq "ELSEWHERE" StatSeq "END"
    | "SWITCH" SWConf
    | "WAIT" "(" PIDExpression ")"
    | "READ" "(" Desig "," Expr0 ")"
    | "READ" "(" Desig ")"
    | "WRITE" "(" Desig "," Expr0 ")"
    | "WRITE" "(" Desig ")"
    | Desig "+=" Desig | Desig "-=" Desig
```

```
      | Desig ":=" Expr0
      | "IF" Relation "THEN" StatSeq "ELSE" StatSeq "END"
      | "IF" Relation "THEN" StatSeq "END"
      | "WHILE" Relation "DO" StatSeq "END"
      | "FOR" "(" Stat ";" Relation ";" Stat ")" "DO" StatSeq "END"

Desig ::= Ident | Desig "[" Expr0 "]"

PIDRelationList ::= PIDRelation "&&" PIDRelationList
                  | PIDRelation "||" PIDRelationList
                  | PIDRelation

PIDRelation ::= PIDExpression "<" PIDExpression
              | PIDExpression "<=" PIDExpression
              | PIDExpression ">" PIDExpression
              | PIDExpression ">=" PIDExpression
              | PIDExpression "==" PIDExpression
              | PIDExpression "!=" PIDExpression

PIDExpression ::= PIDExpression PIDOp PIDExpression | PIDParam

PIDParam ::= "PID" | "HEIGHT" | "WIDTH" | "CORES" | "SNAKEPID"
           | Number | "(" PIDExpression ")" | ε

PIDOp ::= "+" | "-" | "*" | "%" | "/" | ε

SWConf ::= "VOID" | "NS" | "WE" | "NW" | "NE" | "SE" | "SW"
         | "NWS" | "NWE" | "NES" | "ESW" | "NSWE"
         | "N" | "S" | "W" | "E"

Relation ::= Expr0 "<" Expr0 | Expr0 "<=" Expr0 | Expr0 ">" Expr0
           | Expr0 ">=" Expr0 | Expr0 "==" Expr0
           | Expr0 "!=" Expr0 | "(" Relation ")" | Expr0

ExprList ::= Expr0 | Expr0 "," ExprList

Expr0 ::= Expr0 "*" Expr1 | Expr0 "*" Number | Number "*" Expr0
        | Expr0 "/" Number | Expr0 "mod" PIDParam
        | Expr0 "mod" Term | Expr1

Expr1 ::= Expr1 "+" Expr2 | Expr1 "-" Expr2 | Expr2

Expr2 ::= Expr1 "&" Term | Term

Term ::= "NOT" Term | "(" Expr0 ")" | Number | PIDParam | Desig
```

Listing A.1: EBNF for ARMLang.

A.2 Source Code for Some Case Studies

This section presents some selective software implementations which are used in this thesis. At first, Listing A.2 shows the C code for Sparse Matrix Multiplication on the

```
#define _N_ 4
#define _M_ 4

int main (void) {

  int i,j,k,l,d;
  // Sample Initialization of 4x4 Sparse Matrices in Yale Format
  int A[5] = {1,2,3,4,5};
  int lA = 5;
  int IA[5] = {0,2,3,4,5};
  int lIA = 5;
  int JA[5] = {0,3,2,2,0};

  int B[4] = {7,9,8,6};
  int lB = 4;
  int IB[5] = {0,2,2,3,4};
  int lIB = 5;
  int JB[4] = {1,3,1,0};
  int C[4][4] = {0,0,0,0,0,0,0,0,0,0,0,0,0,0,0,0};

  for(i=0;i<_N_;i++){
    for(j=0;j<_M_;j++){
      for(k=IA[i];k<IA[i+1];k++){
        for(l=IB[j];l<IB[j+1];l++){
          if(JA[k]==JB[l])
            C[i][j] = C[i][j] + A[k] * B[l];
        }
      }
    }
  }
  return 0;
}
```

Listing A.2: C code for Sparse Matrix Multiplication in the Yale Sparse Matrix Format.

Microblaze as discussed in Section 5.1.1. Listing A.3 illustrates the corresponding ARMLang code executed on 16 × 16 reconfigurable mesh of Picoblaze cores. I put much effort in optimizing the C version in order to make a fair comparison between the sequential and parallel case. For example, the sparse matrices A and B are statically defined in the C code (an example for a 4×4 matrix is shown in Listing A.2) and, to allow optimal access, A is stored in row compressed format and B is stored in column compressed format. The ARMLang code loads A and B dynamically from memory at startup. This functionality is carried out by the macro function INPUT_16_SLEEP.

```
#include "nn_init.h"
#include "routines.h"
#include "orderings.h"
#define _K_ 2

PROGRAM SparseMM(16:16);
DECLARE
  a  : INTEGER;
  b  : INTEGER;
  c  : INTEGER;
  row : INTEGER;
  myp : INTEGER;
  ta : INTEGER;
  tp : INTEGER;
  topmost : INTEGER;
  t  : INTEGER;
  t2  : INTEGER;
  i  : INTEGER;
  j  : INTEGER
BEGIN
WAIT(1);
SWITCH WE;

INPUT_16_SLEEP(a , t);
INPUT_16_SLEEP(b , t);

// row <- PID%16
row := PID;
row := row/16;
c := 0;
myp:=PID;

FOR(i:=0;i<_K_;i:=i+1) DO
  ta := 0;
  tp := 0;
  t := 0;

  //nonzero nodes split bus
  IF a>0 THEN
    SWITCH N
  ELSE
    SWITCH NS
  END;
  //nonzero nodes broadcast a-value
  IF a>0 THEN
    WRITE(a)
  END;
  SYNC;
  READ(ta);
  //nonzero nodes broadcast PID
  IF a>0 THEN
    WRITE(myp)
  END;
  SYNC;
  READ(tp);
  SYNC;
```

```
  //row0 nodes inform topmost nodes
  WHERE PID<WIDTH DO
    WRITE(tp)
  END;
  SYNC;
  READ(topmost);
  //row0 nodes send values to the
      diagonal nodes
  SWITCH NS;
  WHERE PID<WIDTH DO
    WRITE(ta)
  END;
  SYNC;
  READ(ta);
  WHERE PID<WIDTH DO
    WRITE(tp)
  END;
  SYNC;
  READ(tp);
  //CHECK PID=00
  WHERE PID==0 DO
    IF a==0 THEN
      topmost := 0
    END
  END;
  //Discard A-Element
  IF topmost==myp THEN
    a := 0
  END;
  //Switch to row-buses
  WHERE PID%WIDTH==0 DO
    SWITCH E
  ELSEWHERE
    SWITCH WE
  END;
  //Diagonal nodes broadcast values
  WHERE PID%(WIDTH+1)==0 DO
    WRITE(ta)
  END;
  SYNC;
  READ(ta);
  WHERE PID%(WIDTH+1)==0 DO
    WRITE(tp)
  END;
  SYNC;
  READ(tp);
  ta := ta * b;
  SYNC;
  tp := tp/16;
  FOR(j:=0;j<_K_;j:=j+1) DO
    IF ta>0 THEN
      SWITCH N
    ELSE
      SWITCH NS
    END;
    //row0 nodes inform topmost
        nodes
```

136

```
WHERE PID<WIDTH DO
  topmost := 1;
  WRITE(topmost)
END;
SYNC;
READ(topmost);
SWITCH NS;
//Inform destination PID
IF ta>0 THEN
  IF topmost==1 THEN
    WRITE(tp)
  END
END;
SYNC;
READ(t2);
IF ta>0 THEN
  IF topmost==1 THEN
    WRITE(ta)
  END
END;
SYNC;
READ(t);
```

```
IF t2==row THEN
  c := c + t
END;
//Discard topmost ta
IF ta>0 THEN
  IF topmost==1 THEN
    ta := 0;
    tp := 0
  END
END
END //inner k-loop
END; //gloabal k-loop
SWITCH WE;
OUTPUT_16_SLEEP(c)
END.
```

Listing A.3: ARMLang code for Sparse Matrix Multiplication.

Listing A.4 depicts the the HV-RN self-simulation algorithm that was described in Section 5.3 in full length. The program simulates a sub-mesh of size 2×3 on a single Picoblaze processor. The complexity of the code also shows that self-simulation can lead to a significant overhead. This is due to the fact that, in principle, a self-simulation technique must be applicable to any algorithm of a certain model. But in this specific case, the actual computation is just the addition of six numbers which could definitely be expressed much easier.

```
#define _VOID 0
#define _NS 1
#define _WE 2

PROGRAM submeshsim(1:1);
DECLARE
  data : ARRAY [0..5] OF INTEGER;
  bus  : ARRAY [0..5] OF INTEGER;
  writer : ARRAY [0..5] OF INTEGER;
  pat : ARRAY [0..5] OF INTEGER;
  gpat : ARRAY [0..4] OF INTEGER;
  bdata : INTEGER;
  bwritten : INTEGER;
  lastnode : INTEGER;
  i    : INTEGER
BEGIN
  data[0]:=1; writer[0]:=0;
  pat[0]:=_NS; bus[0]:=0;
  data[1]:=2; writer[1]:=0;
  pat[1]:=_WE; bus[1]:=0;
  data[2]:=3; writer[2]:=1;
```

```
  pat[2]:=_WE; bus[2]:=0;
  data[3]:=4; writer[3]:=1;
  pat[3]:=_NS; bus[3]:=0;
  data[4]:=5; writer[4]:=1;
  pat[4]:=_WE; bus[4]:=0;
  data[5]:=6; writer[5]:=0;
  pat[5]:=_WE; bus[5]:=0;

  // ROW #1
  bwritten := 0;
  gpat[0] := _WE;
  IF pat[0] == _WE THEN
    IF writer[0] == 1 THEN
      bwritten := 1;
      bdata := data[0];
      bus[0] := bdata
    END
  END;
  lastnode := pat[0];
  FOR (i:=1;i<3;i:=i+1) DO
    IF pat[i] == _WE THEN
      IF writer[i] == 1 THEN
```

```
        bwritten := 1;
        bdata   := data[i]
     ELSE
       IF lastnode == _WE THEN
         IF bwritten == 1 THEN
           bus[i] := bdata
         END
       END
     END
   ELSE
     gpat[0] := _VOID
   END;
   lastnode := pat[i]
 END;
 bwritten := 0;
 IF pat[2] == _WE THEN
   IF writer[2] == 1 THEN
     bwritten := 1;
     bdata   := data[2];
     bus[2] := bdata
   END
 END;
 lastnode := pat[2];
 i:=2;
 WHILE(i>0) DO
   i := i-1;
   IF pat[i] == _WE THEN
     IF writer[i] == 1 THEN
       bwritten := 1;
       bdata   := data[i]
     ELSE
       IF lastnode == _WE THEN
         IF bwritten == 1 THEN
           bus[i] := bdata
         END
       END
     END
   ELSE
     gpat[0] := _VOID
   END;
   lastnode := pat[i]
 END;
 // ROW #2
 bwritten := 0;
 gpat[1] := _WE;
 IF pat[3] == _WE THEN
   IF writer[3] == 1 THEN
     bwritten := 1;
     bdata   := data[3];
     bus[3] := bdata
   END
 END;
 lastnode := pat[3];
```

```
 FOR (i:=4;i<6;i:=i+1) DO
   IF pat[i] == _WE THEN
     IF writer[i] == 1 THEN
       bwritten := 1;
       bdata   := data[i]
     ELSE
       IF lastnode == _WE THEN
         IF bwritten == 1 THEN
           bus[i] := bdata
         END
       END
     END
   ELSE
     gpat[1] := _VOID
   END;
   lastnode := pat[i]
 END;
 bwritten := 0;
 IF pat[5] == _WE THEN
   IF writer[5] == 1 THEN
     bwritten := 1;
     bdata   := data[5];
     bus[5] := bdata
   END
 END;
 lastnode := pat[5];
 i:=5;
 WHILE(i>3) DO
   i := i-1;
   IF pat[i] == _WE THEN
     IF writer[i] == 1 THEN
       bwritten := 1;
       bdata   := data[i]
     ELSE
       IF lastnode == _WE THEN
         IF bwritten == 1 THEN
           bus[i] := bdata
         END
       END
     END
   ELSE
     gpat[1] := _VOID
   END;
   lastnode := pat[i]
 END
END .
```

Listing A.4: Self-simulation of a 2×3 mesh on a single processor in ARMLang.

ALU	arithmetic logic unit
ANN	all nearest neighbors
API	application programming interface
AROB	array with reconfigurable optical buses [model]
ASIC	application-specific integrated circuit
AST	abstract syntax tree
BNF	BackusNaur form
BRAM	block random access memory
BSP	bulk synchronous parallel computers [model]
CA	cellular automaton [model]
CAAPP	content addressable array parallel processor [model]
CDL	cellular description language
CMOS	complementary metal oxide semiconductor
CRCW	concurrent read and concurrent write
CREW	concurrent read and exclusive write
DRN	directed reconfigurable mesh [model]
EDK	embedded development kit [tool]
EDT	euclidean distance transform [algorithm]
FF	flip-flop
FIFO	first-in first-out [storage element]
FPGA	field programmable gate array
FR-Mesh	fusing restricted reconfigurable mesh [model]
FSL	fast simplex link [bus interface]
GCN	gated connection network
HDL	hardware design language
HV-RN	horizontal-vertical reconfigurable mesh [model]
ISA	instruction set architecture
ISE	integrated software environment [tool]
IUA	image understanding architecture

JTAG	Joint Test Action Group [debug interface]
KCPSM	constant coded programmable state machine (Picoblaze)
KNN	k-nearest neighbor [algorithm]
LALR	lookahead left to right [parsing]
LMB	local memory bus [bus interface]
LRN	linear reconfigurable mesh [model]
LUT	look-up table
MIMD	multiple-instruction multiple-data
MIPS	microprocessor without interlocked pipeline stages
MPI	message passing interface
MUXCY	carry chains multiplexer
NCD	native circuit description [file format]
NIC	network interface controller
PARBS	processor array with reconfigurable bus system [model]
PE	processing element
PID	processing element ID
PLB	processor local bus [bus interface]
PPA	polymorphic processor array [model]
PPC	polymorphic parallel C [language]
PRAM	parallel random access machine [model]
RAM	random access machine [model]
RAMP	research accelerator for multiple processors
RISC	reduced instruction set computer
RMESH	reconfigurable mesh [one specific model]
RMPC	reconfigurable mesh parallel C [language]
RN	reconfigurable network aka reconfigurable mesh
ROM	read-only memory
SA	systolic array [model]
SE	switch element
SIMD	single-instruction multiple-data
SMM	sparse matrix multiplication
SPMD	single-program multiple-data
VHDL	VHSIC hardware description language
VLIW	very long instruction word
VLSI	very large scale integration
XCL	Xilinx cache link
XMD	Xilinx microprocessor debugger
XPA	Xilinx power analyzer [tool]
XUP	Xilinx university program
YUPPIE	Yorktown ultra parallel polymorphic image engine

Author's Publications

[1] Heiner Giefers and Achim Rettberg. Energy Aware Multiple Clock Domain Scheduling for a Bit-serial, Self-timed Architecture. In *19th Symp. on Integrated Circuits and Systems Design (SBCCI'06)*, Ouro Preto, Brazil, August 2006. ACM.

[2] Heiner Giefers and Marco Platzner. A Many-Core Implementation Based on the Reconfigurable Mesh Model. In *Int. Conf. on Field Programmable Logic and Applications (FPL '07)*, Amsterdam, Netherlands, August 2007. IEEE.

[3] Heiner Giefers and Marco Platzner. Realizing Reconfigurable Mesh Algorithms on Softcore Arrays. In *Int. Symp. on Embedded Computer Systems: Architectures, Modeling and Simulation (IC-SAMOS '08)*, Samos, Greece, July 2008. IEEE.

[4] Heiner Giefers. Reconfigurable Many-Cores with Lean Interconnect. In *Proceedings of the 18th International Conference on Field Programmable Logic and Applications (FPL'08)*, Heidelberg, Germany, September 2008. IEEE. PhD Forum Presentation.

[5] Heiner Giefers and Marco Platzner. Towards Models for Many-Cores: The Case for the Reconfigurable Mesh. In *Int. Conf. on Architecture of Computing Systems (ARCS), Workshop on Many-Cores*, Delft, Netherlands, March 2009. VDE.

[6] Heiner Giefers and Marco Platzner. ARMLang: A Language and Compiler for Programming Reconfigurable Mesh Many-Cores. In *23rd Int. Parallel and Distributed Processing Symp., Reconfigurable Architectures Workshop (RAW '09)*, Rome, Italy, May 2009. IEEE.

[7] Heiner Giefers and Marco Platzner. Program-Driven Fine-Grained Power Management for the Reconfigurable Mesh. In *Int. Conf. on Field Programmable Logic and Applications (FPL '09)*, Prague, Czech Republic, Aug./Sept. 2009. IEEE.

[8] Heiner Giefers and Marco Platzner. A Self-Reconfigurable Lightweight Interconnect for Scalable Processor Fabrics. In *10th Int. Conf. on Engineering of Reconfigurable Systems and Algorithms (ERSA'10)*, Las Vegas, USA, July 2010. CSREA Press.

[9] Heiner Giefers and Marco Platzner. A Triple Hybrid Interconnect for Many-Cores: Reconfigurable Mesh, NoC and Barrier. In *Int. Conf. on Field Programmable Logic and Applications (FPL '10)*, Milano, Italy, Aug./Sept. 2010. IEEE.

Bibliography

[10] Anant Agarwal, Liewei Bao, John Brown, Bruce Edwards, Matt Mattina, Chyi-Chang Miao, Carl Ramey, and David Wentzlaff. The Tile Processor Architecture. Presentation at HOT CHIPS 19, August 2007. Tilera.

[11] Alok Aggarwal and Ashok K. Chandra. Communication complexity of PRAMs. In *15th Int. Colloquium on Automata, Languages and Programming (ICALP '88)*, 1988.

[12] Alok Aggarwal, Ashok L. Chandra, and Marc Snir. On Communication Latency in PRAM Computations. In *1st Symp. on Parallel Algorithms and Architectures (SPAA '89)*, 1989.

[13] B. Alpern, L. Carter, E. Feig, and T. Selker. The Uniform Memory Hierarchy Model of Computation. *Algorithmica*, 12(2–3):72–109, 1994.

[14] Bowen Alpern, Larry Carter, and Jeanne Ferrante. Modeling Parallel Computers as Memory Hierarchies. In *Programming Models for Massively Parallel Computers*, 1993.

[15] Hari Angepat, Dam Sunwoo, and Derek Chiou. RAMP-White: An FPGA-Based Coherent Shared Memory Parallel Computer Emulator. In *8th Annual Austin CAS Conference*, March 2007.

[16] Krste Asanović, Ras Bodik, Bryan Christopher Catanzaro, Joseph James Gebis, Parry Husbands, David A. Patterson Kurt Keutzer and, William Lester Plishker, John Shalf, Samuel Webb Williams, and Katherine A. Yelick. The Landscape of Parallel Computing Research: A View from Berkeley. Technical Report UCB/EECS-2006-183, EECS Department, UC Berkeley, 2006.

[17] Yossi Azar and Uzi Vishkin. Tight comparison bounds on the complexity of parallel sorting. *SIAM Journal on Computing*, 16(3):458–464, 1987.

[18] P. Baglietto, M. Maresca, and M. Migliardi. A Simulator For Reconfigurable Massively Parallel Architectures. In *2nd Euromicro Workshop on Parallel and Distributed Processing*, pages 185–189, January 26-28 1994.

[19] P. Baglietto, M. Maresca, and M. Migliardi. Euclidean distance transform on Polymorphic Processor Array. In *Computer Architectures for Machine Perception (CAMP '95)*, pages 288–293, 18-20 Sept. 1995.

[20] A. Banerjee, R. Mullins, and S. Moore. A Power and Energy Exploration of Network-on-Chip Architectures. In *1st Int. Symp. on Networks-on-Chip (NOCS '07)*, pages 163–172, 2007.

[21] B. Baxter and B. Greer. Apply: A Parallel Compiler for Image Processing Applications. In *Proc. of the 6th Distributed Memory Computing Conference*, 1991.

[22] Paul Beame and Johan Hastad. Optimal bounds for decision problems on the CRCW PRAM. In *19th Symp. on Theory of Computing (STOC '87)*, 1987.

[23] Y. Ben-Asher, D. Gordon, and A. Schuster. Optimal Simulations in Reconfigurable Arrays. Technical Report CS716, Technion - Israel Institute of Technology, 1992.

[24] Y. Ben-Asher, D. Peleg, R. Ramaswami, and A. Schuster. The Power of Reconfiguration. *Journal of Parallel and Distributed Computing*, 13(2):139–153, 1991.

[25] Yosi Ben-Asher, Dan Gordon, and Assaf Schuster. Efficient Self-Simulation Algorithms for Reconfigurable Arrays. *Journal of Parallel and Distributed Computing*, 30(1):1–22, 1995.

[26] Yosi Ben-Asher, David Peleg, and Assaf Schuster. The Complexity of Reconfiguring Network Models. In *Israel Symp. on Theory of Computing Systems*, pages 79–90, 1992.

[27] Yosi Ben-Asher and Assaf Schuster. Time-size tradeoffs for reconfigurable meshes. *Parallel Processing Letters*, 6(2):231–245, 1996.

[28] L. Benini and G. DeMicheli. Networks on Chips: A New SoC Paradigm. *IEEE Computer*, 35(1):70–78, 2002.

[29] Bryan Beresford-Smith, Oliver Diessel, and Hossam ElGindy. Optimal algorithms for constrained reconfigurable meshes. *Journal of Parallel and Distributed Computing*, 39(1):74–78, 1996.

[30] Tobias Bjerregaard and Shankar Mahadevan. A survey of research and practices of Network-on-chip. *ACM Computing Surveys*, 38(1), 2006.

[31] Venkatavasu Bokka, Himabindu Gurla, Stephan Olariu, and James L. Schwing. Constant-time convexity problems on reconfigurable meshes. *Journal of Parallel and Distributed Computing*, 27:86–99, 1995.

[32] M. Bolotski, T. Simon, C. Vieri, R. Amirtharajah, and Jr. T. F. Knight. Abacus: a 1024 processor 8 ns SIMD array. In *16th Conf. on Advanced Research in VLSI (ARVLSI '95)*, page 28, Washington, DC, USA, 1995. IEEE Computer Society.

[33] K. Bondalapati and V. Prasanna. Reconfigurable Meshes: Theory and Practice. In *11th Int. Parallel Processing Symp., Reconfigurable Architectures Workshop (RAW '97)*, 1997.

[34] Olaf Bonorden. *Versatility of Bulk Synchronous Parallel Computing: From the Heterogeneous Cluster to the System on Chip*. PhD thesis, University of Paderborn, 2008.

[35] Olaf Bonorden, Ben Juurlink, Ingo von Otte, and Ingo Rieping. The Paderborn University BSP (PUB) library. *Parallel Computing*, 29(2):187–207, 2003.

[36] S. Borkar, R. Cohn, G. Cox, T. Gross, H.T. Kung, M. Lam, M. Levine, B. Moore, W. Moore, C. Peterson, J. Susman, J. Sutton, J. Urbanski, and J. Webb. Supporting systolic and memory communication in iWarp. In *17th Int. Symp. on Computer Architecture (ISCA '90)*, pages 70–81, 1990.

[37] O. Bouattane, J. Elmesbahi, M. Khaldoun, and A. Rami. A Fast Algorithm for k-Nearest Neighbor Problem on a Reconfigurable Mesh Computer. *Intelligent and Robotic Systems*, 32(3):347–360, 2001.

[38] Richard P. Brent and H. T. Kung. The Area-Time Complexity of Binary Multiplication. *Journal of the ACM*, 28(3):521–534, 1981.

[39] Kuei-Chung Chang, Jih-Sheng Shen, and Tien-Fu Chen. Evaluation and Design Trade-Offs Between Circuit-Switched and Packet-Switched NOCs for Application-Specific SOCs. In *43rd Design Automation Conference (DAC '06)*. ACM, 2006.

[40] Cristian Coarfa, Yuri Dotsenko, John Mellor-Crummey, Franois Cantonnet, Tarek El-Ghazawi, Ashrujit Mohanti, Yiyi Yao, and Daniel Chavarra-Miranda. An Evaluation of Global Address Space Languages: Co-array Fortran and Unified Parallel C. In *10th Symp. on Principles and Practice of Parallel Programming*, 2005.

[41] P. Corsonello, G. Spezzano, G. Staino, and D. Talia. Efficient Implementation of Cellular Algorithms on Reconfigurable Hardware. In *10th Euromicro Workshop on Parallel, Distributed and Network-based Processing*, 2002.

[42] David Culler, Richard Karp, David Patterson, Abhijit Sahay, Klaus Erik Schauser, Eunice Santos, Ramesh Subramonian, and Thorsten von Eicken. LogP: Towards a Realistic Model of Parallel Computation. In *Proc. of the 4th ACM SIGPLAN Symp. on Principles and Practice of Parallel Programming (PPOPP '93)*, pages 1–12, 1993.

[43] Artur Czumaj, Friedhelm Meyer auf der Heide, and Volker Stemann. Simulating shared memory in real time: on the computation power of reconfigurable architectures. *Information and Computation*, 137(2):103–120, 1997.

[44] William J. Dally and Brian Towles. Route Packets, Not Wires: On-Chip Inteconnection Networks. In *38th Design Automation Conference (DAC '01)*, 2001.

[45] Frank Dehne, Andreas Fabri, and Andrew Rau-Chaplin. Scalable Parallel Geometric Algorithms for Coarse Grained Multicomputers. In *Proc. of the 9th Symposium on Computational Geometry (SCG '93)*, pages 298–307, 1993.

[46] Michael deLorimier, Nachiket Kapre, Nikil Mehta, Dominic Rizzo, Ian Eslick, Raphael Rubin, Tomás E. Uribe, Thomas F. Knight Jr, and André DeHon. GraphStep: A System Architecture for Sparse-Graph Algorithms. In *14th Symp. on Field-Programmable Custom Computing Machines (FCCM '06)*, 2006.

[47] Andrew Duller, Daniel Towner, Gajinder Panesar, Alan Gray, and Will Robbins. picoArray Technology: The Tool's Story. In *Design, Automation and Test in Europe Conference and Exhibition (DATE '05)*, pages 106–111, Washington, DC, USA, 2005. IEEE Computer Society.

[48] Stanley Eisenstat, M.C. Gursky, Martin Schultz, and Andrew Sherman. Yale Sparse Matrix Package II. Nonsymmetric Codes. Technical Report YALE/DCS/TR114, Yale University, Department of Computer Science, 1977.

[49] Hossam ElGindy. and Lachlan Wetherall. An L_1 Voronoi Diagram Algorithm for a Reconfigurable Mesh. In *1st Int. Conf. on Algorithms and Architectures for Parallel Processing (ICAP '95)*, volume 1, pages 442–451vol.1, 19-21 April 1995.

[50] Hossam ElGindy. and Lachlan Wetherall. A simple Voronoi diagram algorithm for a reconfigurable mesh. *IEEE Trans. Parallel Distrib. Syst.*, 8(11):1133–1142, 1997.

[51] Hossam A. ElGindy and Paulina Wegrowicz. Selection on the Reconfigurable Mesh. In *Int. Conf. on Parallel Processing (ICPP '91)*, 1991.

[52] J. Elmesbahi. Nearest neighbor problems on a mesh-connected computer. *IEEE Trans. Syst., Man, Cybern.*, 20(5):1199–1204, 1990.

[53] Dan Ernst, Nam Sung Kim, Shidhartha Das, Sanjay Pant, Rajeev Rao, Toan Pham, Conrad Ziesler, David Blaauw, Todd Austin, Krisztian Flautner, and Trevor Mudge. Razor: A Low-Power Pipeline Based on Circuit-Level Timing Speculation. In *36th IEEE/ACM Int. Symp. on Microarchitecture (MICRO-36)*, 2003.

[54] Mary M. Eshaghian-Wilner and Lili Hai. An Optically Interconnected Reconfigurable Mesh. *Journal of Parallel and Distributed Computing*, 61(6):737–747, 2001.

[55] Mary M. Eshaghian-Wilner, Alex Khitun, Shiva Navab, and Kang L. Wang. A Nano-Scale Reconfigurable Mesh with Spin Waves. In *3rd Conf. on Computing Frontiers (CF '06)*, volume 2006, pages 65–69, 2006.

[56] Mary M. Eshaghian-Wilner, Alex Khitun, Shiva Navab, and Kang L. Wang. A Nano-Scale Architecture for Constant Time Image Processing. *Phys. Status Solidi A*, 204(6):1931–1936, 2007.

[57] Mary M. Eshaghian-Wilner, Alex Khitun, Shiva Navab, and Kang L. Wang. The Spin-Wave Nanoscale Reconfigurable Mesh and the Labeling Problem. *ACM Journal on Emerging Technologies in Computing Systems*, 3(2), 2007.

[58] Mary M. Eshaghian-Wilner, Ling Lau, Shiva Navab, and David Shen. Graph Formations of Partial-Order Multiple-Sequence Alignments Using Nanoscale, Microscale, and Multiscale Reconfigurable Meshes. *IEEE Trans. Nanobiosci.*, 8(3):201–209, 2009.

[59] A. Estrella-Balderrama, J.A. Fernandez-Zepeda, and A.G. Bourgeois. Fault tolerance and scalability of the reconfigurable mesh. In *18th Int. Parallel and Distributed Processing Symp. (IPDPS '04)*, page 172, 26-30 April 2004.

[60] Ricardo Fabbri, Luciano Da F. Costa, Julio C. Torelli, and Odemir M. Bruno. 2D Euclidean distance transform algorithms: A comparative survey. *ACM Computing Surveys*, 40(1):1–44, 2008.

[61] J.A. Fernndez-Zepeda, R. Vaidyanathan, and J.L. Trahan. Scaling simulation of the fusing-restricted reconfigurable mesh. *IEEE Trans. Parallel Distrib. Syst.*, 9(9):861–871, 1998.

[62] Jos Alberto Fernndez-Zepeda, Ramachandran Vaidyanathan, and Jerry L. Trahan. Improved Scaling Simulation of the General Reconfigurable Mesh. In *13th Int. Parallel Processing Symp. & 10th Symp. on Parallel and Distributed Processing (IPPS/SPDP '99)*, pages 616–624, London, UK, 1999. Springer-Verlag.

[63] Steven Fortune and James Wyllie. Parallelism in random access machines. In *10th Symp. on Theory of Computing (STOC'78)*, 1978.

[64] Terry J. Fountain and Vartkes Goetcherian. Clip 4 parallel processing system. *IEE Proceedings - Computers and Digital Techniques*, 127(5):219–224, 1980.

[65] Terry J. Fountain, K. N. Matthews, and Michael J. B. Duff. The CLIP7A Image Processor. *IEEE Trans. Pattern Anal. Machine Intell.*, 10(3):310–319, 1988.

[66] A. Gara, M. A. Blumrich, D. Chen, G. L.-T. Chiu, P. Coteus, M. E. Giampapa, R. A. Haring, P. Heidelberger, D. Hoenicke, G. V. Kopcsay, T. A. Liebsch, M. Ohmacht, B. D. Steinmacher-Burow, T. Takken, and P. Vranas. Overview of the Blue Gene/L system architecture. *IBM Journal of Research and Development*, 49(2):195–212, 2005.

[67] Phillip B. Gibbons. A More Practical PRAM Model. In *1st Symp. on Parallel Algorithms and Architectures (SPAA '89)*, 1989.

[68] T. Gross, S. Hinrichs, D.R. O'Hallaron, T. Stricker, and A. Hasegawa. Communication styles for parallel systems. *IEEE Computer*, 27(12):34–44, 1994.

[69] Thomas Gross, A. Hasegawa, Susan Hinrichs, David O"Hallaron, and Thomas Stricker. The Impact of Communication Style on Machine Resource Usage for the iWarp Parallel Processor. Technical report, Carnegie Mellon University, Pittsburgh, PA, USA, 1992.

[70] Pierre Guerrier and Alain Greiner. A Generic Architecture for On-Chip Packet-Switched Interconnections. In *Design, Automation and Test in Europe Conference and Exhibition (DATE '00)*, 2000.

[71] Mathias Halbach and Rolf Hoffmann. Implementing Cellular Automata in FPGA Logic. In *18th Int. Parallel and Distributed Processing Symp. (IPDPS '04)*, 2004.

[72] Eric Hao, Philip D. Mackenzie, and Quentin F. Stout. Selection on the Reconfigurable Mesh. In *4th Symp. on the Frontiers of Massively Parallel Computation (Frontiers '92)*, pages 38–45, 19-21 Oct. 1992.

[73] Wolfgang Heenes, Rolf Hoffmann, and Sebastian Kanthak. FPGA Implementations of the Massively Parallel GCA Model. In *19th Int. Parallel and Distributed Processing Symp., Workshop Proceedings (IPDPS '05)*, 2005.

[74] Jonathan M. D. Hill, Bill McColl, Dan C. Stefanescu, Mark W. Goudreau, Kevin Lang, Satish B. Rao, Torsten Suel, Thanasis Tsantilas, and Rob H. Bisseling. BSPlib: The BSP programming library. *Parallel Computing*, 24(14):1947–1980, 1998.

[75] Christian Hochberger and Rolf Hoffmann. CDL - a language for cellular processing. In *2nd Int. Conf. on Massively Parallel Computing Systems*, 1996.

[76] Rolf Hoffmann, Klaus-Peter Völkmann, Stefan Waldschmidt, and Wolfgang Heenes. GCA: Global Cellular Automata. A Flexible Parallel Model. In *6th Int. Conf. on Parallel Computing Technologies (PaCT '01)*, 2001.

[77] Yatin Hoskote, Sriram Vangal, Arvind Singh, Nitin Borkar, and Shekhar Borkar. A 5-GHz Mesh Interconnect for a Teraflops Processor. *IEEE Micro*, 27(5):51–61, 2007.

[78] J. Jang, H. Park, and V. K. Prasanna. A bit model of reconfigurable mesh. In *6th Int. Parallel Processing Symp., Reconfigurable Architectures Workshop (RAW '92)*, 1992.

[79] Jin-Wook Jang, Madhusudan Nigam, Viktor K. Prasanna, and Sartaj Sahni. Constant time algorithms for computational geometry on the reconfigurable mesh. *IEEE Trans. Parallel Distrib. Syst.*, 8(1):1–12, Jan. 1997.

[80] Ju-Wook Jang, Heonchul Park, and Viktor K. Prasanna. An Optimal Multiplication Algorithm on Reconfigurable Mesh. *IEEE Trans. Parallel Distrib. Syst.*, 8(5):521–532, 1997.

[81] Ju-Wook Jang, Heonchul Park, and V.K. Prasanna. A fast algorithm for computing a histogram on reconfigurable mesh. *IEEE Trans. Pattern Anal. Machine Intell.*, 17(2):97–106, Feb. 1995.

[82] Ju-Wook Jang and Viktor K. Prasanna. An optimal sorting algorithm on reconfigurable mesh. *Journal of Parallel and Distributed Computing*, 25(1):31–41, 1995.

[83] S. Kelem, S. Box, S. snd Wasson, R. Plunkett, J. Hassoun, and Phillips C. An Elemental Computing Architecture for SD Radio. In *Software Defined Radio Technical Conference*, Denver, Colorado, November 5-9 2007.

[84] Ken Kennedy, Charles Koelbel, and Hans Zima. The rise and fall of High Performance Fortran: an historical object lesson. In *3rd Conf. on History of Programming Languages (HOPL III)*, 2007.

[85] D. Kissler, F. Hannig, A. Kupriyanov, and J. Teich. A highly parameterizable parallel processor array architecture. In *Int. Conf. on Field Programmable Technology (ICFPT '06)*, pages 105–112, Dec. 2006.

[86] Donald E. Knuth. *The Art of Computer Programming Vol. 3, Sorting and Searching*. Addison-Wesley, 1998.

[87] Cornelis H. A. Koster. *Compiler Construction: An Advanced Course*, chapter Using the CDL Compiler-Compiler, pages 366–426. Springer, 1976.

[88] Alex Krasnov, Andrew Schultz, John Wawrzynek, Greg Gibeling, and Pierre-Yves Droz. RAMP Blue: A Message-Passing Manycore System in FPGAs. In *Int. Conf. on Field Programmable Logic and Applications (FPL '07)*, pages 54–61, 2007.

[89] V. K. Prasanna Kumar and C. S. Raghavendra. Array processor with multiple broadcasting. In *12th Int. Symp. on Computer Architecture (ISCA '85)*, 1985.

[90] H. T. Kung. Why Systolic Architectures? *IEEE Computer*, 15(1):37–46, 1982.

[91] H. T. Kung and Charles E. Leiserson. Systolic Arrays (for VLSI). In *Symp. on Sparse Matrix Comput.*, 1978.

[92] Monica S. Lam and Robert P. Wilson. Limits of control flow on parallelism. In *19th Int. Symp. on Computer Architecture (ISCA '92)*, 1992.

[93] Walter Lee, Rajeev Barua, Matthew Frank, Devabhaktuni Srikrishna, Jonathan Babb, Vivek Sarkar, and Saman Amarasinghe. Space-time scheduling of instruction-level parallelism on a raw machine. In *8th Int. Conf. on Architectural Support for Programming Languages and Operating Systems (ASPLOS-VIII)*, pages 46–57, New York, NY, USA, 1998. ACM.

[94] F. Thomson Leighton. Tight bounds on the complexity of parallel sorting. In *16th Symp. on Theory of Computing (STOC '84)*, 1984.

[95] F. Thomson Leighton. *Introduction to Parallel Algorithms and Architectures: Array, Trees, Hypercubes.* Morgan Kaufmann, 1991.

[96] H. Li and M. Maresca. Polymorphic-Torus Architecture for Computer Vision. *IEEE Trans. Pattern Anal. Machine Intell.*, 11(3):233–243, 1989.

[97] H. Li and M. Maresca. Polymorphic-Torus Network. *IEEE Trans. Comput.*, 38(9):1345–1351, 1989.

[98] Zhiyong Li, Peter H. Mills, and John H. Reif. Models and Resource Metrics for Parallel and Distributed Computation. In *28th. Int. Conf. on System Sciences*, 1995.

[99] Jian Liang, Andrew Laffely, Sriram Srinivasan, and Russell Tessier. An architecture and compiler for scalable on-chip communication. *IEEE Trans. VLSI Syst.*, 12(7):711–726, 2004.

[100] Rong Lin, Stephan Olariu, James L. Schwing, and Jingyuan Zhang. Sorting in $O(1)$ time on an $n \times n$ reconfigurable mesh. In *9th European Workshop on Parallel Computing*, 1992.

[101] Radu Marculescu, Umit Y. Ogras, Li-Shiuan Peh, Natalie Enright Jerger, and Yatin Hoskote. Outstanding Research Problems in NoC Design: System, Microarchitecture, and Circuit Perspectives. *IEEE Trans. Computer-Aided Design*, 28(1):3–21, 2009.

[102] M. Maresca. Polymorphic processor arrays. *IEEE Trans. Parallel Distrib. Syst.*, 4(5):490–506, 1993.

[103] M. Maresca and P. Baglietto. A Programming Model for Reconfigurable Mesh based Parallel Computers. In *Programming Models for Massively Parallel Computers*, pages 124–133, 1993.

[104] M. Maresca and H. Li. Connection autonomy in SIMD computers: a VLSI implementation. *Journal of Parallel and Distributed Computing*, 7(2):302–320, 1989.

[105] Massimo Maresca and Hungwen Li. *Reconfigurable Massively Parallel Computers*, chapter Polymorphic VLSI arrays with distributed control, pages 33–63. Prentice Hall, 1991.

[106] Norman Margolus. An FPGA architecture for DRAM-based systolic computations. In *Symp. on FPGAs for Custom Computing Machines (FCCM '97)*, 1997.

[107] Gary C. Marsden, Philippe J. Marchand, Phil Harvey, and Sadik C. Esener. Optical transpose interconnection system architectures. *Optics Letters*, 18(13):1083–1085, 1993.

[108] MathStar. Field Programmable Object Arrays - An Overview. White Paper, August 2004.

[109] Susumu Matsumae and Nobuki Tokura. An efficient self-simulation algorithm for reconfigurable meshes. In *12th Symp. on Parallel Algorithms and Architectures (SPAA '00)*, pages 216–223, 2000.

[110] K. N. Matthew. *The CLIP7 Image Analyser–A multi-bit processor array*. PhD thesis, Univ. of London, 1986.

[111] Ciaran McIvor, Máire McLoone, and John V. McCanny. High-Radix Systolic Modular Multiplication on Reconfigurable Hardware. In *Int. Conf. on Field Programmable Technology (ICFPT '05)*, 2005.

[112] Martin Middendorf, Hartmut Schmeck, Heiko Schröder, and Gavin Turner. Multiplication of Matrices With Different Sparseness Properties on Dynamically Reconfigurable Meshes. *VLSI Design*, 9(1):69–81, 1999.

[113] R. Miller, V.K. Prasanna-Kumar, D.I. Reisis, and Q.F. Stout. Parallel Computations on Reconfigurable Meshes. *IEEE Trans. Comput.*, 42(6):678–692, 1993.

[114] Russ Miller, V. K. Prasanna-Kumar, Dionisios Reisis, and Quentin F. Stout. Meshes with reconfigurable buses. In *5th MIT Conf. on Advanced research in VLSI*, pages 163–178, Cambridge, MA, USA, 1988. MIT Press.

[115] Russ Miller and Quentin F. Stout. Mesh computer algorithms for computational geometry. *IEEE Trans. Comput.*, 28(3):321–340, 1989.

[116] M. Mirza-Aghatabar, S. Koohi, S. Hessabi, and M. Pedram. An Empirical Investigation of Mesh and Torus NoC Topologies Under Different Routing Algorithms and Traffic Models. In *Euromicro Symp. on Digital System Design (DSD '07)*, 2007.

[117] Kensuke Miyashita and Reiji Hashimoto. A Java Applet to Visualize Algorithms on Reconfigurable Mesh. In *14th Int. Parallel and Distributed Processing Symp., Workshop Proceedings (IPDPS '00)*, pages 137–142, 2000.

[118] Trevor Mudge. Power: A First-Class Architectural Design Constraint. *IEEE Computer*, 34(4):52–58, 2001.

[119] M. Manzur Murshed and Richard P. Brent. RMSIM: A Serial Simulator for Reconfigurable Mesh Parallel Computers. Technical Report TR-CS-97-06, The Australian National University, 1997.

[120] Manzur Murshed and Richard P. Brent. Adaptive AT2 optimal algorithms on reconfigurable meshes. *Parallel Computing*, 26(11):1447–1458, 2000.

[121] Manzur Murshed and Richard P. Brent. How Promising is the k-Constrained Reconfigurable Mesh? In *15th Int. Conf. on Computers and Their Applications*, pages 288–291, 2000.

[122] M.M. Murshed and R.P. Brent. Serial simulation of reconfigurable mesh, an image understanding architecture. *Advances in Computer Cybernetics*, 5:92–97, 1998.

[123] S. Murtaza, A. G. Hoekstra, and P. M. A. Sloot. Compute Bound and I/O Bound Cellular Automata Simulations on FPGA Logic. *ACM Transactions on Reconfigurable Technology and Systems*, 1(4):23:1–23:21, 2009.

[124] Syed Murtaza. *High performance reconfigurable computing with cellular automata.* PhD thesis, University of Amsterdam, 2010.

[125] David Nassimi and Sartaj Sahni. Bitonic Sort on a Mesh-Connected Parallel Computer. *IEEE Trans. Comput.*, 28(1):2–7, 1979.

[126] M. Nigam and S. Sahni. Sorting n Numbers on $n \times n$ Reconfigurable Meshes with Buses. In *7th Int. Parallel Processing Symp. (IPPS '93)*, pages 174–181, 13-16 April 1993.

[127] Stephan Olariu and James L. Schwing. A novel deterministic sampling scheme with applications to broadcast-efficient sorting on the reconfigurable mesh. *Journal of Parallel and Distributed Computing*, 32:215–222, 1996.

[128] Stephan Olariu, James L. Schwing, and Jingyuan Zhang. On the Power of Two-Dimensional Processor Arrays with Reconfigurable Bus Systems. *Parallel Processing Letters*, 1(1):29–34, 1991.

[129] Stephan Olariu, James L. Schwing, and Jingyuan Zhang. Integer Problems on Reconfigurable Meshes, with Applications. *Journal of Computer and Software Engineering*, 1:33–46, 1993.

[130] Stephan Olariu, James L. Schwing, and Jingyuan Zhang. Optimal convex hull algorithms on enhanced meshes. *BIT Numerical Mathematics*, 33(3):396–410, 1993.

[131] Y. Pan, M. Hamdi, and K. Li. Euclidean distance transform for binary images on reconfigurable mesh-connected computers. *IEEE Trans. Syst., Man, Cybern. B*, 30(1):240–244, 2000.

[132] Yi Pan and Mounir Hamdi. Quicksort on a Linear Array with a Reconfigurable Pipelined Bus System. In *Int. Symp. on Parallel Architectures*, 1996.

[133] Partha Pratim Pande, C. Grecu, M. Jones, A. Ivanov, and R. Saleh. Performance Evaluation and Design Trade-Offs for Network-on-Chip Interconnect Architectures. *IEEE Trans. Comput.*, 54(8):1025–1040, 2005.

[134] Gajinder Panesar, Daniel Towner, Andrew Duller, Alan Gray, and Will Robbins. Deterministic Parallel Processing. *Int. Journal of Parallel Programming*, 34(4):323–341, 2006.

[135] Heonchul Park, Hyoung Joong Kim, and Viktor K. Prasanna. An O(1) time optimal algorithm for multiplying matrices on reconfigurable mesh. *Information Processing Letters*, 47(2):109–113, 1993.

[136] Heonchul Park, Viktor K. Prasanna, and Ju wook Jang. Fast Arithmetic on Reconfigurable Meshes. In *Int. Conf. on Parallel Processing (ICPP '93)*, 1993.

[137] Arun Patel, Christopher A. Madill, Manuel Saldana, Christopher Comis, Regis Pomes, and Paul Chow. A Scalable FPGA-based Multiprocessor. In *14th Symp. on Field-Programmable Custom Computing Machines (FCCM '06)*, pages 111–120, 2006.

[138] Sandy Pavel and Selim G. Akl. On the Power of Arrays with Reconfigurable Optical Buses. Technical report, Department of Computing and Information Science, Queen's University, Kingston, Ontario, Canada, 1995.

[139] C. Peterson, J. Sutton, and P. Wiley. iWarp: a 100-MOPS, LIW microprocessor for multicomputers. *IEEE Micro*, 11(3):26–29, 1991.

[140] Manuel Saldana and Paul Chow. TMD-MPI: An MPI Implementation for Multiple Processors Across Multiple FPGAs. In *Int. Conf. on Field Programmable Logic and Applications (FPL '06)*, pages 1–6, 2006.

[141] Manuel Saldana, Lesley Shannon, and Paul Chow. The routability of multiprocessor network topologies in FPGAs. In *SLIP '06: Proceedings of the 2006 international workshop on System-level interconnect prediction*, pages 49–56, New York, NY, USA, 2006. ACM.

[142] Isaac D. Scherson and Sandeep Sen. Parallel sorting in two-dimensional VLSI models of computation. *IEEE Trans. Comput.*, 38(2):238–249, 1989.

[143] Claus-Peter Schnorr and Adi Shamir. An optimal sorting algorithm for mesh connected computers. In *18th Symp. on Theory of Computing (STOC '86)*, 1986.

[144] Friedrich Wilhelm Schrer. *The GENTLE Compiler Construction System*. R. Oldenbourg, 1997.

[145] Assaf Shacham, Keren Bergman, and Luca P. Carloni. Photonic Networks-on-Chip for Future Generations of Chip Multiprocessors . *IEEE Trans. Comput.*, 57(9):1246–1260, 2008.

[146] Barry Shackleford, Motoo Tanaka, Richard J. Carter, and Greg Snider. FPGA Implementation of Neighborhood-of-Four Cellular Automata Random Number Generators. In *10th Int. Symp. on Field Programmable Gate Arrays (FPGA '02)*, 2002.

[147] David Shoemaker, Frank Honore, Chris Metcalf, and Steve Ward. NuMesh: an architecture optimized for scheduled communication. *Journal of Supercomputing*, 10(3):285–302, 1996.

[148] D. B. Shu, J. G. Nash, and K. Kim. Parallel Implementation of Image Understanding Tasks on Gated-Connection Networks. In *5th Int. Parallel Processing Symp. (IPPS '91)*, 1991.

[149] L. Snyder. Introduction to the Configurable, Highly Parallel Computer. *IEEE Computer*, 15(1):47–56, 1982.

[150] Carsten Steckel, Martin Middendorf, Hossam A. ElGindy, and Hartmut Schmeck. A Simulator for the Reconfigurable Mesh Architecture. In *Parallel and Distributed Processing, 10th IPPS/SPDP '98 Workshops*, pages 99–104, 1998.

[151] Quentin F. Stout. Mesh-Connected Computers with Broadcasting. *IEEE Trans. Comput.*, C-32(9):826–830, 1983.

[152] Kang Sun, Jun Zheng, Yuanyuan Li, and Xuezeng Pan. Design of a Simulator for Mesh-Based Reconfigurable Architectures. In *Int. Conf. on Network and Parallel Computing*, 2007.

[153] M.B. Taylor, J. Kim, J. Miller, D. Wentzlaff, F. Ghodrat, B. Greenwald, H. Hoffman, P. Johnson, Jae-Wook Lee, W. Lee, A. Ma, A. Saraf, M. Seneski, N. Shnidman, V. Strumpen, M. Frank, S. Amarasinghe, and A. Agarwal. The Raw microprocessor: a computational fabric for software circuits and general-purpose programs. *IEEE Micro*, 22(2):25–35, March-April 2002.

[154] C. D. Thompson and H. T. Kung. Sorting on a mesh-connected parallel computer. *Communications of the ACM*, 20(4):263–271, 1977.

[155] Clark D. Thompson. The VLSI Complexity of Sorting. *IEEE Trans. Comput.*, C-32(12):1171–1184, 1983.

[156] Tilera Corporation. Tile Processor Architecture. Technology Brief, August 2007.

[157] César Torres-Huitzil and Miguel Arias-Estrada. Real-time image processing with a compact FPGA-based systolic architecture. *Real-Time Imaging*, 10:177–187, 2004.

[158] Jerry L. Trahan, Chun-Ming Lu, and Ramachandran Vaidyanathan. Integer and Floating Point Matrix-Vector Multiplication on the Reconfigurable Mesh. In *10th Int. Parallel Processing Symp. (IPPS '96)*, 1996.

[159] Ramachandran Vaidyanathan and Jerry L. Trahan. *Dynamic Reconfiguration*. Springer, 2004.

[160] Ramachandran Vaidyanathan, Jerry L. Trahan, and Chun-Ming Lu. Degree of scalability: scalable reconfigurable mesh algorithms for multiple addition and matrix-vector multiplication. *Parallel Computing*, 29(1):95–109, 2003.

[161] Leslie G. Valiant. A Bridging Model for Parallel Computation. *Communications of the ACM*, 33(8):103 –111, 1990.

[162] D. Vantrease, R. Schreiber, M. Monchiero, M. McLaren, N. P. Jouppi, M. Fiorentino, A. Davis, N. Binkert, R. G. Beausoleil, and J. H. Ahn. Corona: System Implications of Emerging Nanophotonic Technology. In *35th Int. Symp. on Computer Architecture (ISCA '08)*, 2008.

[163] Stamatis Vassiliadis and Ioannis Sourdis. FLUX interconnection networks on demand. *Journal of Systems Architecture*, 53(10):777–793, 2007.

[164] Uzi Vishkin. Using Simple Abstraction to Reinvent Computing for Parallelism. *Communications of the ACM*, 54:75–85, 2011.

[165] Uzi Vishkin, George C. Caragea, and Bryant Lee. *Handbook of Parallel Computing*, chapter Models for Advancing PRAM and Other Algorithms into Parallel Programs for a PRAM-On-Chip platform. CRC Press, 2008.

[166] John von Neumann. *Theory of Self-Reproducing Automata*. University of Illinois Press, Champaign, IL, USA, 1966.

[167] E. Waingold, M. Taylor, D. Srikrishna, V. Sarkar, W. Lee, V. Lee, J. Kim, M. Frank, P. Finch, R. Barua, J. Babb, S. Amarasinghe, and A. Agarwal. Baring it all to software: Raw machines. *IEEE Computer*, 30(9):86–93, 1997.

[168] B.-F. Wang and G.-H. Chen. Constant Time Algorithms for the Transitive Closure and Some Related Graph Problems on Processor Arrays with Reconfigurable Bus Systems. *IEEE Trans. Parallel Distrib. Syst.*, 1(4):500–507, 1990.

[169] Biing-Feng Wang and Gen-Haey Chen. Two-dimensional processor array with a reconfigurable bus system is at least as powerful as CRCW model. *Information Processing Letters*, 36(1):31–36, 1990.

[170] Biing-Feng Wang, Gen-Huey Chen, and Hungwen Li. Configurational Computation: A New Computation Method on Processor Arrays with Reconfigurable Bus Systems. In *Int. Conf. on Parallel Processing (ICPP '91)*, pages 42–49, 1991.

[171] Biing-Feng Wang, Gen-Huey Chen, and Ferng-Ching Lin. Constant time sorting on a processor array with a reconfigurable bus system. *Information Processing Letters*, 34(2):187–192, 1990.

[172] Qiang Wang, Subodh Gupta, and Jason Anderson. Clock Power Reduction for Virtex-5 FPGAs. In *17th Int. Symp. on Field Programmable Gate Arrays (FPGA '09)*, 2009.

[173] John Wawrzynek, David Patterson, Mark Oskin, Shih-Lien Lu, Christoforos Kozyrakis, James C. Hoe, Derek Chiou, and Krste Asanović. RAMP: Research Accelerator for Multiple Processors. *IEEE Micro*, 27(2):46–57, 2007.

[174] Sewook Wee, Jared Casper, Njuguna Njoroge, Yuriy Tesylar, Daxia Ge, Christos Kozyrakis, and Kunle Olukotun. A practical FPGA-based framework for novel CMP research. In *15th Int. Symp. on Field Programmable Gate Arrays (FPGA '07)*, pages 116–125, New York, NY, USA, 2007. ACM.

[175] C.C. Weems, S. Levitan, A.R. Hanson, E.M. Riseman, J.G. Nash, and D. Shu. The Image Understanding Architecture. *Int. Journal of Computer Vision*, 2(3):252–282, 1989.

[176] Charles C. Weems, Edward M. Riseman, Allen R. Hanson, P.J. Narayanan, Ling Tony Chen, Larry S. Davis, Leah H. Jamieson, Edward J. Delp, Chao-Chun Wang, Juan Li, and Frank J. Weil. Image Understanding Architecture: Exploiting Potential Parallelism in Machine Vision. *IEEE Computer*, 25(2):65–77, 1992.

[177] Xingzhi Wen and Uzi Vishkin. FPGA-Based Prototype of a PRAM-On-Chip Processor. In *5th Conf. on Computing Frontiers (CF '08)*, 2008.

[178] David Wentzlaff, Patrick Griffin, Henry Hoffmann, Liewei Bao, Bruce Edwards, Carl Ramey, Matthew Mattina, Chyi-Chang Miao, John F. Brown III, and Anant Agarwal. On-Chip Interconnection Architecture of the Tile Processor. *IEEE Micro*, 27(5):15–31, 2007.

[179] D. Wiklund and Dake Liu. SoCBUS: switched network on chip for hard real time embedded systems. In *17th Int. Parallel and Distributed Processing Symp. (IPDPS '03)*, pages 8 pp.–, 2003.

[180] J. Williams and N. Bergmann. Programmable parallel coprocessor architectures for reconfigurable system-on-chip. In *Int. Conf. on Field Programmable Technology (ICFPT '04)*, pages 193–200, 2004.

[181] J.A. Williams, I. Syed, J. Wu, and N.W. Bergmann. A Reconfigurable Cluster-on-Chip Architecture with MPI Communication Layer. In *14th Symp. on Field-Programmable Custom Computing Machines (FCCM '06)*, pages 350–352, 2006.

[182] Stephen Wolfram. Twenty Problems in the Theory of Cellular Automata. *Physica Scripta*, 1985(T9):170, 1985.

[183] P.T. Wolkotte, G.J.M. Smit, G.K. Rauwerda, and L.T. Smit. An Energy-Efficient Reconfigurable Circuit-Switched Network-on-Chip. In *19th Int. Parallel and Distributed Processing Symp. (IPDPS '05)*, pages 155a–155a, 04-08 April 2005.

[184] Xilinx Inc. Virtex-II Pro and Virtex-II Pro X Platform FPGAs: Complete Data Sheet. Data Sheet, Nov. 2007. DS083.

[185] Xilinx, Inc. PicoBlaze 8-bit Embedded Microcontroller User Guide. UG129, June 2008.

[186] Xilinx, Inc. *MicroBlaze Processor Reference Guide (v11.2)*, UG081 (v11.2) edition, Sep 2010.

[187] Zhihua Yu, Fengguang Luo, Bin LI, Weilin Zhou, Liangjia Zong, and Qing Tao. Reconfigurable mesh-based inter-chip optical interconnection network for distributed-memory multiprocessor system. *Optik*, 121(20):1845–1847, 2010.